ב"ה

A GUIDE TO GOOD HEALTH

Healthy in Body, Mind and Spirit

Based on the Teachings of
The Lubavitcher Rebbe
Rabbi Menachem M. Schneerson

GENERAL THEMES AND SUBJECTS RELATING TO HEALTH

VOLUME I

by Rabbi Sholom B. Wineberg

Sichos In English
788 Eastern Parkway
Brooklyn, New York, 11213

היתשס"ה • 2005

Healthy in Body, Mind and Spirit
Volume I

Published and Copyrighted © by
Sichos In English
788 Eastern Parkway • Brooklyn, N.Y. 11213
Tel. (718) 778-5436

ISBN 1-8814-0078-6

5765 • 2005

CREDITS
Rochel Chana Schilder for editing.
Yosef Yitzchok Turner for designing the layout and typography.
Rabbi Yonah Avtzon for preparing text for publication.
Avrohom Weg for designing the cover.
Uri Kaploun for editorial assistance.

TABLE OF CONTENTS

COMPILER'S FOREWORD

Based on linguistic evidence, it would appear that life and good health is almost a Jewish preoccupation.

For a start, what is the most familiar Jewish toast? *LeChayim!* (Literally, "To life!")

If someone wants to say, "No worries; keep it and enjoy," how does he say that inYiddish? He says, *Zol zain tzu gizunt!* ("Let it just add to your health!")

With what words does one farewell a friend? *Zai mir gizunt!* ("Do me a favor and stay healthy!").

And if a Yiddish-speaker wants to reassure an anxious friend that the best thing to do about a passing crisis is to view it in perspective and ignore it, he simply says, *Abi gizunt!* ("As long as you have your health!")

A Jew, then, is constantly concerned about a life of good health – and rightly so, from both a physical and a spiritual standpoint.

* * *

In the annals of Jewish history, no individual has so frequently been turned to for counsel and blessings regarding this critical issue as the Lubavitcher Rebbe. Hence the veritable mountain of responses and statements that offer guidance on this subject — through his voluminous correspondence, through answers relayed via his secretariat, and through public pronouncements at the chassidic gatherings known as *farbrengens*.

This volume, the first of three entitled *Healthy in Body, Mind and Spirit,* presents a broad, representative selection of the Rebbe's advice and insights on physical and mental health. The present volume deals with health issues of a general nature, while volumes two and three deal with more specific issues of physical and mental health.

Since, as the Rebbe so often indicated, the spiritual and physical health of a Jew are inexorably intertwined, many of the Rebbe's responses and comments also relate to a Jew's spiritual well-being. However, the present compilation does not address problems and issues that are strictly spiritual in nature, even when these issues may well spark repercussions in the clinical sphere.

True, the Rebbe's approach to healing was holistic. The Rebbe would take into consideration the physical, mental and spiritual dimensions of an ailment or of the ailing individual and would advise accordingly.

At the same time, the Rebbe drew a clear line between the physical and spiritual aspects of healing. The physical aspect of healing was invariably dealt with in an entirely medical manner, while the spiritual aspect — such as checking *mezuzos* and *tefillin* — was not intended to serve as a substitute for what was to be done within the confines of nature.

An example: In two public talks[1] the Rebbe stated emphatically that in a choice between two doctors, one of whom is an acknowledged expert but is not necessarily G-d-fearing, while the other is less expert but more G-d-fearing, Jewish law directs the patient to the more competent physician. Healing a patient, the Rebbe explained, is an issue of *pikuach nefesh*, a matter of life and death. And what counts here is the doctor's expertise, not his religiosity.

On other occasions, the Rebbe voiced a similar sentiment by recounting the following incident[2] about the circumcision of one of the grandsons of the third Lubavitcher Rebbe, the *Tzemach*

---

1. *Sichos Kodesh 5737*, Vol. I, p. 172ff.; *op. cit.*, p. 340ff.
2. *Likkutei Sichos*, Vol. I, p. 33. See also *Toras Menachem 5711*, Vol. I, p. 278.

Tzedek. There was a choice between two circumcisors — one *mohel* was a venerable chassid whose meditations were steeped in the Kabbalistic *kavanos* of the famed mystic, Rabbi Yitzchak Luria, while the other *mohel,* a younger man, was a renowned expert, but not at all as learned.

The *Tzemach Tzedek* advised that the younger man be chosen. In this world, he explained, the essential element of a *mitzvah* is its actual, physical execution.[3] In this case, therefore, the critical criterion ought to be: Who of the two candidates for the required task would do it more deftly?

* * *

Most of the material assembled in this work consists of private responses to individuals. It must therefore be borne in mind that the Rebbe's answer to one individual does not necessarily apply at all to another, for, as the Rebbe once wrote,[4] "It is *patently obvious*[5] that a directive to an *individual* does not serve *at all* as a directive to the public, even when the issues are the same."

Moreover, some of the responses to individuals are not necessarily the Rebbe's final word on the matter, particularly since the Rebbe would encourage the use of the latest medical advances, procedures and medications, some of which were not extant at the time he offered those responses.

What we have done to try to resolve this latter difficulty is to quote numerous responses, even though some may appear different from others. The dates or sources cited may be of benefit in distinguishing the Rebbe's later responses. So, too, by noting that numerous answers are written in the same vein, we have an indication of the Rebbe's overall approach to a specific issue or matter.

---

3. In the original Heb./Aram., *asiyah le'eila.*
4. In a handwritten response.
5. Emphasis is the Rebbe's.

In addition, the Rebbe sometimes referred to medical issues at public *farbrengens*. Many of his directives appear in these volumes. The Rebbe's public directives in the course of the year 5748 (1988) are particularly noteworthy, such as the following:

"The general response to the questions many people [ask me] regarding medical matters: Follow the advice of an expert doctor;[6] better yet, the advice of two expert doctors. Should they disagree, a third doctor should be consulted and the majority opinion should be followed."[7]

At a *farbrengen* less than a week later, the Rebbe added the following: "On questions of health and healing, there is the commandment and instruction of the Torah, 'Scrupulously guard your health,'[8] [which is accomplished] by following the instructions of the doctor; better yet, a doctor who is also [the patient's] *friend,* for then he is truly interested in his welfare, and so on.

"... Moreover, and this is of great importance: By being truly connected (*hiskashrus amitis*) to the *Nasi HaDor* (i.e., the spiritual head of the generation), [which is accomplished both] by studying his Torah teachings and — in the realm of action — by following in his ways and paths, and so on, *in the*

---

6. This is based on the Torah's directive, "and he shall heal" (*Shmos* 21:19). On this the *Gemara* comments: "From this we learn that permission was granted to the doctor to heal" (*Berachos,* foot of p. 60a) — and "permission" also bears the sense of *empowering* the healer. This, too, falls within the category of *pikuach nefesh,* saving a life (*Shulchan Aruch, Yoreh Deah,* beg. of sec. 336).

   A person in need of healing is commanded by the Torah to seek healing. We derive this from the verse, "Scrupulously guard your health" (*Devarim* 4:15). This has been expounded on at length, particularly in *Hilchos Nizkei Guf veNefesh* and in *Hilchos Shmiras Guf veNefesh* in the *Shulchan Aruch* of R. Yosef Caro — and some of these laws are also to be found in the *Shulchan Aruch* of the Alter Rebbe.

7. *Sefer HaSichos 5748,* p. 240.

8. *Va'eschanan* 4:15. See also *Berachos,* foot of p. 32b, and *Chiddushei Aggados Maharsha* there.

best possible manner, then ... there will be no need to consult doctors, since the healing will come from G-d *Himself* (and not through a mortal doctor). For when 'I am G-d, your Healer,'[9] then from the very outset 'no illness... will befall you.' "[10] ...

Studying the Rebbe's answers and talks on matters of health in itself forges another link in one's personal spiritual bond with the Rebbe. And in itself, as stated above, such study constitutes a positive step towards sound health.

Knowledge of the Rebbe's directives on healing also echoes the theme of a letter that the Rebbe wrote before accepting the mantle of leadership. There he writes, with regard to the Previous Rebbe:[11] "There is a Rebbe among the Jewish people, and he is not bound at all by the limitations of nature. A person who wishes to proceed on a secure path with regard to crucial life decisions should not lift his hand without asking the Rebbe. When a person is confused or confronted by fundamental life questions, he must know that the Jewish people have not been left without succor. There is someone to ask....

"He should not rely solely on his own understanding ..., nor on the doctor. ...These are approaches that involve doubt. He has a sure path where he can clarify his doubts.... And when he follows [the Rebbe's] directives, he will succeed."

* * *

To conclude on a personal note: This volume is dedicated to my dear friend, Reb Nochum Noach ben Esther *sheyichyeh*. May G-d grant him a complete and speedy recovery.

May our study of these volumes of the Rebbe's teachings and directives strengthen our continued spiritual bond with him, and

9. *Shmos* 15:26.
10. *Ibid.*
11. *Igros Kodesh*, Vol. III, p. 52ff.

enable us to merit "the all-encompassing healing that will come in the Ultimate Future, in the era of *Mashiach;* may he come speedily in our days."[12]

Sholom B. Wineberg
Overland Park, Kansas

24th of Teves, 5765
Yahrtzeit of the Alter Rebbe

---

12. *Op. cit.,* Vol. II, p. 27.

CHAPTER 1

The Importance of
Maintaining Good Health

"SEE HOW PRECIOUS IS THE BODY OF A JEW"

... My father-in-law, the Rebbe, of blessed memory, related the statement of his father, the Rebbe [Rashab] *Nishmaso Eden*: "See how precious is the body of a Jew — for its sake has [G-d] poured forth so much [Torah and *mitzvos*]."

When G-d gives each and every one of us something as precious as the body, we are to make every effort and truly exert ourselves to insure that the body be healthy. In so doing, we make it possible to fulfill G-d's will [of performing Torah and *mitzvos*, which is specifically performed with the body].

This is as the *Rambam* states in *Hilchos Deos*, beginning of ch. 4, that "maintaining a healthy and whole body is an integral part of [one's] Divine service." And then there is the letter of *HaRav HaMaggid* [of Mezritch] (printed in *HaTamim*) to his son, the holy "*Malach*," [in which he states]: "A small hole in the body causes a large hole in the soul."[1]

My intent is not to lecture — rather, it is my hope that the above will hopefully have a positive effect on you, and through you [it will also have an effect] upon your husband.

Although the *Zohar* does state[2] that the "strength of the soul leads to the weakening of the body," this is to be understood [in the context of the spiritual power and potency of the holy soul]

1. *HaTamim*, Vol. VII, p. 29.
2. See *Zohar* I, p. 170b.

1

weakening the corporeal demands of the body — not, Heaven forbid, weakening the health of the body.

Indeed, we readily observe that when a person is healthy he can accomplish so much more in all areas [than when he is unhealthy,] particularly with regard to matters relating to love of G-d, love of Torah and love of a fellow Jew. ...

(Igros Kodesh, Vol. IV, p. 341)

"SCRUPULOUSLY GUARD YOUR HEALTH"

I received information about the way you have been conducting yourself. Understandably, it pains me to hear this — if the information is accurate.

By this I mean: I was told that you do a lot of fasting, and that though your family, *sheyichyu,* has been asking and begging you to visit a doctor for your health, you do not take their words to heart; you do not fulfill the doctor's instructions [that you previously received]; [and] you do not even want to seek a doctor's advice [concerning that which ails you now].

Surely I need not go on at length about that which we were commanded:[3] "Scrupulously guard your health." [Nor is it necessary] to expound at length on the words of the Great Teacher, the *Rambam,* in his *Yad HaChazakah, Hilchos Deos,* that "it is impossible to grow in comprehension and wisdom when one is hungry or ill ... for his body must be healthy and whole to serve G-d" (see there the conclusion of ch. 3 and the beginning of ch. 4).

Moreover, when it comes to matters of health, "Permission was granted the healer to heal,"[4] for which reason there are many rulings in *Shulchan Aruch Hilchos Shabbos* and *Hilchos Yom*

---

3.   *Devarim* 4:15.
4.   *Berachos* 60a.

HaKippurim, etc., [relating to the necessity of following the instructions of a physician].

... It is my hope that these few lines will get you to change your conduct to the degree necessary: that you will visit a doctor and follow his instructions precisely. ...

(*Igros Kodesh*, Vol. XVII, p. 96)

THE PARTICULAR IMPORTANCE OF MAINTAINING GOOD HEALTH DURING PRESENT TIMES

We read in the Torah portion of *Mishpatim*:[5] "When you see the donkey of your enemy lying under its load, you may [be tempted] to refrain from helping him, [but] you must come to its aid."

The Baal Shem Tov explains[6] that "donkey" — in Hebrew, *chamor*, from the root *chomer*, materialism — refers to the person's body — "your donkey." When you carefully examine "your donkey," you will see that it is "your enemy": — the body is considered the soul's enemy, as the soul longs for G-dliness and the spiritual, while the body longs for the material and corporeal.

The Baal Shem Tov goes on to say that this "donkey" is "lying under its load" placed upon it by G-d, namely, the "load" of becoming refined through Torah and *mitzvos*. It may then occur to you that "you may [be tempted] to refrain from helping it" by following the path of mortifications and self-torment, thereby "breaking" the body.

However, concludes the Baal Shem Tov, not with this approach will the light of Torah reside. Rather, "you must come to its aid." One may not rely on fasts and other forms of self-mortification to demolish the body's desire for coarse materialism.

---

5. *Shemos* 23:5.
6. *HaYom Yom*, entry for *Shvat* 28; *Kesser Shem Tov (Kehot)* addendum, sec. 16. See also *Ki Sireh Chamor* 5704 (*Sefer HaMaamarim 5704*, p. 145).

Rather, the person should "come to [the body's] aid," by purifying, refining and sanctifying it. In no way should it be subjected to torture and mortification.

The Mezritcher Maggid, the Baal Shem Tov's successor, instructed his son (known as the "Angel" because of his great piety and detachment from all physical matters) that he should scrupulously guard his health, for "A small hole in the body causes a large hole in the soul."[7]

The prohibition against tormenting and causing anguish to one's body is clearly established in Jewish law. Thus the Alter Rebbe states in his Code of Jewish Law[8] that "man does not have ownership over his body, and therefore he may not torment it even [with a minor torment such as] denying it any type of food or drink."

Moreover, the *Rambam*[9] goes so far as to say that maintaining "a healthy and whole body is part of Divine service." Thus, not only is self-mortification prohibited, we are also to take measures — as part of our spiritual service — to ensure that our bodies are "healthy and whole."

What innovation, then, lies in the Baal Shem Tov's commentary on the words "you must come to its aid"? Why in the first place would we entertain thoughts of responding to our "enemy," [the body,] with fasts and other forms of self-mortification?

This will be understood in light of what the Alter Rebbe goes on to say in his Code, that it is permissible to afflict one's body and fast for the purposes of repentance. We may do so since fasting for the sake of repentance ultimately benefits the body, as repentance enables the body to fulfill its Divine mission on earth.

---

7. *HaTamim*, Vol. VII, p. 28.
8. *Shulchan Aruch, Choshen Mishpat, Hilchos Nizkei HaGuf*, para. 4.
9. Beginning of ch. 4 of *Hilchos Deos*.

The Baal Shem Tov's novel interpretation on the verse "you must come to its aid" will be understood accordingly. It is possible, says the Baal Shem Tov, to refine the body and come to its aid — even when it is in need of repentance and spiritual cleansing — not necessarily through mortification but by the positive means of purification and refinement.

This innovative approach was specifically stated by the Baal Shem Tov since the aspects and teachings of *Chassidus* — and the Baal Shem Tov was, after all, the founder of the chassidic movement — are a precursor to and a foretaste of that which will be revealed in the Time to Come, with the arrival of *Mashiach*.

At that time the soul will derive its spiritual nurture from the body. Consequently, now as well, during the latter days of exile, *Chassidus* teaches us that many things can be accomplished with the body not necessarily through mortification, but by the positive manner of refining it with the method of "coming to its aid" [by purifying and refining the body].

This also explains why the importance of a healthy body was given much greater emphasis in later generations. For the later the generation, the closer the time to *Mashiach's* imminent arrival; a time when the latent spirituality found within the body will come to the fore, nurturing and sustaining its soul. As such, special care must be given to the body and it should be accorded an additional measure of respect.

There is also a special quality to a Jewish body,[10] for it is specifically regarding the [Jew's] body that the Torah states:[11] "You have chosen us from among all nations and tongues." *Absolute* freedom of choice is uniquely Divine, and G-d chose the Jewish body. Understandably, "G-d's choice" should be treated with the proper respect.

---

10. *Tanya*, ch. 49. See also *Toras Shalom*, p. 120ff.
11. Text of the morning *Birchas Kerias Shema*.

In addition to the special quality of the body resulting from the body being G-d's choice, *Chassidus* demonstrated a new path in Divine service: that safeguarding one's health can and should be maintained even when spiritual cleansing and repentance are absolutely necessary.

(Based on *Likkutei Sichos*, Vol. II, pp. 530-532)

GOOD HEALTH IS MOST IMPORTANT DURING PRESENT TIMES PRIOR TO MASHIACH'S ARRIVAL

It pleases me to receive news about you from time to time. May G-d help that the tidings I receive about you be good not only in the spiritual sense but also in the physical sense, [i.e., that you are in good health].

For a Jew, good spiritual health and good physical health go hand in hand, as in the well-known saying of the *Rambam*, that "maintaining a healthy and whole body is an integral part of Divine service."

Also, there is the commentary of the Baal Shem Tov on the verse:[12] "When you see the donkey of your enemy lying under its load, you may [be tempted] to refrain from helping him, [but] you must come to its aid," that one is to serve G-d not with fasts and mortifications, but "*with* the body" — "Know G-d in all *your* ways."[13]

If this is so at all times, how much more so during the present time when there are — comparatively — very few people whose work involves disseminating Torah and *mitzvos*. Therefore, each individual who does this work is so precious, and every good deed [he does] is ever so precious.

[It is thus even more important during the present time to be in good health,] for we readily observe that when the body is

---

12. *Shemos* 23:5.
13. *Mishlei* 3:6.

weakened, the soul's effect on the individual is lessened, since the soul works through the body, as explained in *Tanya*, ch. 37, see there.

I initially reckoned that to an individual like yourself I need not go on at length about this. However, I have received reports that you are not taking adequate care of your health — as explained above — and the verse explicitly states:[14] "Scrupulously guard your health."

I am sure that your not paying adequate attention to your health is with the best of intentions, but as mentioned above, nowadays each one of us is a soldier who must obey [the] commands and directives [of the Commander].

Since we have been informed that "in these times, when the approaching footsteps of *Mashiach* are close upon us, the principal service of G-d is the service of charity and [good] deeds" (see *Iggeres HaKodesh* of the Alter Rebbe, conclusion of Epistle IX), we must do all we can to make sure that we have the physical strength to do as much as possible.

Because of this, there is the directive that I heard from my father-in-law, the Rebbe our *Nasi*, which he gave to so many individuals, to have a bite to eat before morning prayers. Moreover, he instructed many individuals not only to have a nibble, but also to have some form of pastry in order to feel stronger, and moreover, to be able to pray with added concentration.

Surely you also know about the famous letter that the Baal Shem Tov wrote to his disciple, the *Baal Toldos Yaakov Yosef*, where he frowns upon engaging in frequent fasts (printed in *HaTamim*, Vol. I, *Ginzei Nistaros* 1:8, *et al.*).

I thank you in advance for writing me that at least from now on you will begin conducting yourself according to the directive of

---

14. *Devarim* 4:15.

my father-in-law, the Rebbe, of blessed memory, that one should guard one's health. As a result, the health of the soul and its Divine service will increase as well.

[With regard to your fasting,] replace it with giving *tzedakah* and a *taanis dibbur*, [i.e., "fasting" from speaking extraneous words] and the like (see *Toldos HaMaharash*, p. 72).[15]

Continue as well your work for the holy institutions in general and *Collel Chabad* in particular — but do so in a manner that will not overstress your body. Conducting yourself this way will be beneficial for the work as well, for then you will have more strength to carry out your work.

It is my strong hope that acting in this manner will enable you to see much success within a very short time, and you will be able to convey [to me news] about your successes for many long years.

(Igros Kodesh, Vol. XIV, p. 327)

"HEALTHY AND WHOLE" — IN BODY AND SPIRIT

... One of the mainstays of Divine service is "You shall come to [the body's] aid" — [i.e., serve G-d] with the body. That is to say, since Divine service is to be healthy and whole, [and man must serve G-d with both body and soul,] it stands to reason that the body must be healthy and whole as well.

This is particularly so, since Jews are "One nation on earth" in their ability to draw down G-d's unity even within physical matters. As such, not only does their spirit conquer their corporeality, but they also transform the corporeal into spirituality, so that there be true unity between the physical and the spiritual.

With blessings that you be able to convey glad tidings of openly revealed goodness regarding all the above.

(Igros Kodesh, Vol. XIV, p. 147)

---

15. In English translation, *Sefer HaToldos Admur Maharash,* SIE, p. 20.

PHYSICAL HEALTH FACILITATES SPIRITUAL HEALTH

I trust that this letter finds you in good health and in good spirits — something that is also relevant to the holiday of Shavuos, [when G-d gave the Torah to the Jewish people]. For, as our Sages, of blessed memory, tell us, before G-d gave the Torah to the Jewish people at Sinai, all those who were in ill health were cured and revitalized.

This [aspect of achieving physical good health prior to receiving the Torah] is also eminently logical, since a physically healthy Jew can better comprehend and follow the Torah and *mitzvos*, thereby accomplishing all that he is required to accomplish.

It thus follows that a Jew is duty-bound to take care of his health, since the health of the Divine soul depends largely on the health of the body, as both, [a healthy soul and a healthy body,] are essential in order to achieve the maximum [required and expected of the Jew].

(From a letter of the Rebbe, dated erev Shavuos, 5735)

SERIOUSNESS OF TAKING CARE OF ONE'S HEALTH

I received your letter and *pidyon nefesh* (prayer request) and will read it at an auspicious time at the *tziyun*, the sacred resting place, of my father-in-law, the Rebbe.

I believe I have already written to you that you need to be more careful in guarding your physical health. Thus you are to be strict in following the doctor's orders and not take them lightly ["*v'loi la'asos 'kuntzen' bazeh*"], for [guarding one's health] is also part of our holy Torah and is a *mitzvah* similar to all other *mitzvos*.

[Moreover,] there is the well-known saying of the Alter Rebbe (quoted in *HaYom Yom*, entry for *erev* Rosh HaShanah): "We have absolutely no conception of how precious a Jew's body is to G-d" — and that which is stated many times in *Chassidus* needs no further proof [of its veracity].

When some people say that they are "*mehadrin*," [i.e., they observe *mitzvos* in the most scrupulous and beautiful manner,] and that is why they are not careful in guarding their health — in truth, such conduct is the very opposite of scrupulous observance.

Conduct yourself in the above manner [of taking care of your health], and G-d will grant you material as well as spiritual good health.

(*Igros Kodesh*, Vol. VII, p. 349)

SUCCEEDING IN ONE'S LABORS
IS CONNECTED TO GOOD HEALTH[16]

Regarding your health situation — do not take it to heart.

However, [make sure to take care of your health, as] guarding our health is an integral part of Divine service,[17] and we are thus obligated to do so. Moreover, this has an impact on our work as well. Thus for the very sake of the success of our work, we are to guard our health.

(*Likkutei Sichos*, Vol. XXXIX, p. 236)

IMPORTANCE OF MAINTAINING GOOD HEALTH

In the beginning, any spiritual arousal is mostly [passion and] light, which is why a person [in such a state will] experience excitement and an increased sense of vitality. The intent [of such an arousal], however, is to bring about actual deed, and to do so on a daily basis — that is to say, to clothe the light [and passion] in vessels [of deeds and actions].

---

16. This letter is the Rebbe's response to a director of a Torah institution who wrote to the Rebbe that the institution's current difficulties have had a negative impact on his physical health and have caused him to become despondent.

17. See *Rambam, Hilchos Deos*, beginning of ch. 4.

Consequently, it is absolutely necessary that the passion be de-emphasized and the vitality be experienced on a lesser level — because [the emphasis must be on] the actual deed. This [actual deed and] performance is the ultimate intent.

Do not listen to the temptations of the evil inclination which claims that the [loss of spiritual passion, arousal and vitality] should lead a person to a state of depression, G-d forbid. Rather, serve G-d in an orderly and ever-increasing manner, clothing the light [and passion] in many vessels [of actual deed].

The progressive growth in matters of holiness follows the message of the verse: "I will banish [the evil and increase in goodness and holiness] little by little."[18] This [progressive growth] applies both to Torah study as well as the performance of *mitzvos* (among them — love of a fellow Jew), not taking on everything all at once or making a giant leap, [but progressing "little by little,"] {except in unique circumstances}.

In order to achieve all the above, the body must be healthy, which is why one must conduct himself in a manner harmonious with a proper diet, [good] sleep, etc. This is in keeping with the expression in *Tanya*, ch. 7: "If one eats fat beef ... in order to broaden his mind [for the service of G-d, then the vitality of the meat ascends to G-d] ... like a burnt offering and sacrifice."

Since it is the "Torah [that] has granted permission to the healer [to heal,]" it follows that when there is a matter of uncertainty regarding a matter of health, or when one is suffering from an ailment, then the doctor should be consulted and his directives followed. ...

(*Igros Kodesh*, Vol. XI, p. 182)

WHEN NECESSARY TAKE A BREAK

In conjunction with what you write in your letter:

---

18. *Shemos* 23:30.

Surely I need not encourage you once again about the importance of obeying the Torah's commandment of guarding one's health, which is also explained in the *maamar* of *Basi LeGani* of *Yud Shevat* of this year,[19] and in many other places. Something as patently obvious as the above does not require additional proofs.

Thus your Torah study or Torah thoughts should be accomplished in a manner that will not have any negative effects on your health.

Do not fool yourself by saying that [minimizing Torah study out of a concern for one's] health emanates from the evil inclination — although at times this may indeed be so. Generally, however, the commandment of "Know G-d in all your ways,"[20] includes the important principle that one is to be in robust and sound physical health.

Therefore, when you feel yourself becoming tired while studying or mentally reviewing your studies, either shift to some other area of study, or take a short break in your studies.

Aside from the fact that taking a break is a *mitzvah* as mentioned above [— since by doing so you are guarding your health—] it also directly relates to the *mitzvah* of Torah study, as it acts as a preparatory step for your subsequent Torah study, enabling you to continue your Torah studies. Moreover, in many regards, the "preparation to a *mitzvah* is likened to the *mitzvah* itself."

(Igros Kodesh, Vol. IX, p. 57)

---

19. *Basi LeGani* 5713, ch. 6 (*Sefer HaMaamarim Melukat* I, p. 34), first printed in 5714, the year this letter was written.
20. *Mishlei* 3:6.

A PROPER SCHEDULE IN ACCORDANCE
WITH ONE'S HEALTH REQUIREMENTS

I received your letter in which you write about the state of your health:

You should seek the counsel of your spiritual mentor (*mashpia*), asking him to arrange your course of studies so that it will not in any way negatively impact your health, for there is the known Torah ruling,[21] "Maintaining a healthy and whole body is an integral part of Divine service."

Surely you are also aware of the saying of the Alter Rebbe (quoted in *HaYom Yom*, entry for *erev* Rosh HaShanah): "We have absolutely no conception of how precious the body of a Jew is to G-d."

You should therefore follow the doctor's orders and make sure to follow a proper schedule — in accordance with your health requirements — regarding food, drink and rest. G-d will then also grant you success that your *davening* and Torah study be accomplished with proper Divine reverence (*Yiras Shamayim*).

Enclosed is the *maamar*[22] where you will also see that the spiritual deficiency caused by the power of the body only refers to the body being dominated by the animal soul, but not — G-d forbid — regarding the [power of the body] in relation to a person's health, for that is related to the well-being of the Divine soul.

(*Igros Kodesh*, Vol. VIII, p. 141)

NO VALID EXCUSES FOR NOT PROPERLY
TAKING CARE OF ONE'S HEALTH

... Since there are those who complain that you claim you are not properly caring for your health because of the negative impact

---

21. *Rambam, Hilchos Deos*, beginning of ch. 4.
22. *Basi LeGani 5713*.

this would have on your work for the *Yeshivah*, [as it would take away time, etc.], [I must therefore note the following]:

It is well known that any and all such excuses have no validity when used to oppose the Code of Jewish Law. Nor are these excuses justifiable when opposing, as they do, the rulings of the Baal Shem Tov, the Maggid, the Alter Rebbe, and the *Nesiim* who followed, who were all extremely strict regarding guarding one's health.

This is also cited briefly — brief in comparison to the importance of this matter — in the *maamar* of *Yud Shevat* 5713.

Since [taking proper care of one's health] is demanded of us by our *Nesiim*, it surely will not result in any damage regarding a *mitzvah* in general, and particularly with regard to the *Yeshivah*. On the contrary, "One *mitzvah* brings about another,"[23] thereby benefiting the *Yeshivah* as well.

I surely need not expound further. ...

(Igros Kodesh, Vol. VIII, p. 309)

PRAYING FOR GOOD HEALTH

... In reply to your question as to whether it is proper to fervently pray for success in material matters, etc., as well as good health.

Your question, understandably, is astonishing, as we are commanded in our Torah, the Torah of Life, to "Scrupulously guard your health," and the *Rambam* rules in *Hilchos Deos*, the conclusion of ch. 3 and the beginning of ch. 4, that a person must see to it that he be healthy and robust.

There is also a ruling that, in general, a person must guard his health and all aspects [of his being]; and to quote the Alter Rebbe in his *Shulchan Aruch*, *Hilchos Nizkei Guf v'Nefesh v'Dineihem*,

---

23. *Avos* 4:2.

para. 4: "A person has no rights at all over his body ... to torment it with any sort of pain...." See there as well in *Hilchos Shmiras Guf*. I need not elaborate further on something that is already well known.

Moreover, according to many *Rishonim*, when a person feels that he is lacking something; e.g., health, etc., it is a positive commandment of the Torah to pray to G-d for that which he needs.

(Igros Kodesh, Vol. XIX, p. 122)

A FLORIDA VACATION FOR BODY AND SOUL

I received with pleasure and joy your letter of Monday, *Parshas Chayei Sarah*. I was already concerned that I had not heard from you for a while, although I was partly mollified by the letter that I received from your son *sheyichye*, which contained regards from you.

I am pleased that you found a residence [in Florida], and I hope that you and your wife *tichye* will feel good there and be able to use the time to truly strengthen your physical health, which for a Jew also leads to health of the soul.

As the Maggid of Mezritch wrote to his son, Reb Avraham the "*Malach*" — who very much followed the course of fasting and self-mortification, and in general was detached from this corporeal world and whose father would often try to convince him not to serve G-d in this manner — "A small hole in the body causes a large hole in the soul."[24]

We readily observe this with our own eyes: that those individuals who desire to serve G-d — and their bodies do not interfere by being weak and the like — are able to serve Him in a more complete manner.

---

24. *HaTamim*, Vol. VII, p. 29.

In addition to the above, it is also explained in many *sefarim* that the body is not a person's possession, but belongs to G-d. Therefore a person must take care of himself and see that his body is in good condition (understandably not at the expense of damaging his soul).

This is also why, according to Jewish law, a person who inflicts injury on himself, although he is not subject to punishment in a human court of law, is guilty according to the laws of Heaven.

In the words of the Alter Rebbe:[25] "A person has no rights at all over his body, neither to smite it, nor to shame it, nor to torment it with any sort of pain, unless he does so as a form of repentance, for this pain [for the sake of repentance] is doing the person a service — to save himself from *Gehinnom*."

I hope that you will soon find a circle of friends there upon whom you will be able to exert an influence, so that they will become not only physically healthy in Florida, but spiritually [healthy] as well.

(Igros Kodesh, Vol. V, p. 59)

IMPORTANCE OF GOOD HEALTH, PARTICULARLY FOR HAVING CHILDREN

... You surely remember that when [the two of] you were here, I repeatedly told your husband, the *Rav shlita*, to take care and be meticulous regarding [receiving sufficient] nourishment and regarding his health in general.

For in addition to the main aspect that this is a command of our holy Torah — in the words of the *Rambam:* "Maintaining a healthy and whole body is an integral part of Divine service" — it is also relevant to your particular situation of [desiring] to have children.

---

25. *Shulchan Aruch, Hilchos Nizkei Guf v'Nefesh v'Dineihem,* para. 4.

During our conversation I noticed that he was not taking the matter [of his health] too seriously, so I reiterated my words, and from the time that the two of you have returned to the Holy Land, I have become even more apprehensive that he is taking this matter all too lightly and is not watching over [his diet and health] at all.

My intent [of the words] "watching over" is very simple — that your husband receive from a doctor a routine and a schedule for his meals as well as a list of healthy and good foods, and [that he do the same] regarding all other matters that are important to good health.

Hopefully, at least from now on, your husband will do the above; it does not matter if he will only do so under duress (*v'lu yehei b'kabbalos ol*), as long as it comes to pass. And nothing stands in the way of will — if he but wills it, he will do it.

(Igros Kodesh, Vol. XVIII, p. 50)

AS IN ALL MATTERS OF TORAH AND MITZVOS
HEALTH SHOULD PROGRESS "FROM GOOD TO BETTER"

I received your letter of *erev Shabbos Kodesh Nachamu*:

Thank G-d for the news that your health has improved; surely it will continue to keep improving — as is the case of all matters of holiness [where one should constantly improve his spiritual condition,] for a Jew's health is also a matter of holiness.

This is as my father-in-law, the Rebbe, הכ״מ, stated several times in the name of his father, the Rebbe [Rashab] *Nishmaso Eden*: "See how precious the body of a Jew is [to G-d] — for its sake has [G-d] poured forth so much [Torah and *mitzvos*]." [It thus follows that the health of one's body] must constantly increase and improve.

Moreover, it is also important for a Jew to be healthy so that [the opposite of good health will] not act — Heaven forbid — as a hindrance to his study of Torah and performance of Divine service.

(Igros Kodesh, Vol. III, p. 398)

THE SACRED JEWISH BODY

I have been receiving information about your state of health. My hope is that today is better than yesterday and tomorrow will be better still. For we have been commanded by G-d to "Ascend in holiness,"[26] and the Jewish body is sacred.

Known as well are the words of the Alter Rebbe in his holy *Tanya*, ch. 49: " 'And You have chosen us from among all nations and tongues' — this refers to the material body."

(Igros Kodesh, Vol. XV, p. 100)

"G-D'S HEALING" — THE BEST CURATIVE

... May G-d will it that in the future you will be able to convey only glad tidings about matters whose goodness is openly revealed, and so, too, with regard to matters of health — that [in the future may] your healing come about specifically in a manner of "G-d's healing," as the verse states:[27] "For I am G-d your healer," for which reason "no illness —from the very outset[28] — shall befall you."[29] ...

(Igros Kodesh, Vol. XV, p. 276)

---

26. *Yoma* 12b, *et al.*

27. *Shemos* 15:26.

28. This is in accordance with the simple meaning of the text and the commentaries of *Rashi* and the *Ramban*, for which reason this interpretation does not conflict with the *Midrashic* understanding of the verse stated in *Sanhedrin* 101a.

29. *Ibid.*

CHAPTER 2

Proper Nutritional Routine
and Leading
a Healthful Lifestyle

THE IMPACT OF GOOD HEALTH AND A
POSITIVE FRAME OF MIND ON ONE'S FAMILY

I was shocked to have received information that [regarding the manner of your spiritual service] you are conducting yourself in unusual and irregular ways and paths; [you are fasting, are not properly safeguarding your health, and are conducting yourself in a reclusive and non-joyous manner].

All this notwithstanding the fact that all are aware of the well-trodden path of our holy Rebbeim, of blessed memory, as well as that which is explained in the revealed portion of Torah — explained as well by the *Rambam* in *Hilchos Deos*[1] — that the "middle path," [i.e., not going to extremes,] is the proper and good path.

Chassidus explains at great length that G-d should be served with joy, and that "you must come to [the body's] aid"[2] — to serve G-d with the body and not through self-mortification and fasting. This has already been expounded on in many places, especially in the *sichos* where it has been expounded upon at length.

---

1. 1:4.
2. *Shemos* 23:5.

This is all the more so when G-d has blessed you with the gift of marriage — your obligation then extends not only to yourself but to another Jewish soul as well; it is only by succeeding in your marriage that you will merit that the Divine Presence resides in your midst.

This being so, it goes without saying that you must guard your health in order to fulfill the three obligations of a husband to his wife, [i.e., those of sustenance, clothing and marital relations,] and to serve G-d with joy and gladness of heart — which fundamentally also includes simply bringing joy to the household, which is achieved by acting in a kind and gentle manner. Surely I need not go on at length about [such] a simple and obvious matter.

If you were to follow my opinion, you would follow the "royal road" that was provided to us by our Rebbeim and *Nesiim*. Abandon the path of fasting, self-mortification, withdrawal and the like.

May G-d bless you that you be able to serve Him with both body and soul, and the joy of fulfilling the *mitzvos* will shatter and eliminate all [internal] boundaries and limitations that seek to hinder this form of service.

(Igros Kodesh, Vol. X, p. 187)

PROPER RESPECT FOR ONE'S HEALTH

... I was pained by the information I received that you look gaunt and haggard (*mareh panav iz nit bazunder frei'end*).

It seems that you have once again begun your path of torment and self-mortification and disregard for your health, even though you are aware of the *Rambam's* ruling in *Hilchos Deos*, beginning of ch. 4, that "maintaining a healthy and whole body is an integral part of Divine service."

Also known is the ruling quoted in *Shulchan Aruch Rabbeinu HaZakein, Hilchos Nizkei Guf v'Nefesh*, para. 4: "An individual has no rights at all over his body to smite it, shame it, or cause it any form of pain, even with regard to food and drink — unless he does so as a form of repentance, at which time he is doing the body a service."

Since the Alter Rebbe has already stated in *Iggeres HaTeshuvah*[3] that during present generations the path of repentance is not through fasting but through other methods, the ruling of the Alter Rebbe in his *Shulchan Aruch* (*Shulchano HaTahor*) remains standing, [that it is forbidden to mortify the body by denying it food and drink].

[This idea of] not listening to what you were told [(by me) about taking care of your health] and only desiring to do that which is right according to *your* understanding [of it], must cease.

Surely you also saw the letter of the Baal Shem Tov — printed in *HaTamim* — to his disciple, the author of the *Toldos* [where he writes that he was extremely upset to hear that he was engaging in frequent fasts, etc.].

I await good news with regard to all the above.

(*Igros Kodesh*, Vol. VI, p. 168)

A WEAKENED BODY HINDERS ONE'S SPIRITUAL SERVICE

I was astounded to learn of your daily schedule, a schedule that is not in keeping with the proper manner of protecting G-d's possessions, i.e., one's body.[4]

This is particularly so in light of that which has been explained at length in *maamarim* and many *sichos* that maintaining good health is part of one's Divine service, and the manner of

---

3. Ch. 3.
4. See *Shulchan Aruch Rabbeinu HaZakein, ibid.* Also in *Rambam, Hilchos Rotzeiach* 1:4, and commentary of *Radbaz, ibid., Hilchos Sanhedrin* 18:6.

one's spiritual service must specifically be that of assisting the body and utilizing it for Divine service, rather than negating the body [through neglecting its basic needs].

This applies to an even greater extent in our generation, as people are not as strong as they used to be (see *Iggeres HaTeshuvah*, beginning of ch. 3). For we readily observe that when the body is weakened, it first and foremost hinders one's service of prayer. Moreover, it also hinders a person's Torah study and even his performance of *mitzvos*.

Consequently, in almost all instances, afflicting oneself (*sigufim*) invariably causes more harm than benefit. I certainly don't need to expound at length about a matter that has already been amply elucidated.

It is my strong hope that upon receiving this letter, you will cease starving yourself until late in the day. Rather, you should drink a beverage that strengthens the body and eat some form of pastry as well — and [this should be done] even prior to the [morning] prayers.

There is also the already famous aphorism of our holy Rebbeim and their directive that: "One should eat in order to be able to pray, rather than pray in order to be able to eat."

Their intent is to be taken literally as well, that if one is hungry during the time of prayer, then it is impossible — for people like us — for it not to affect our concentration during prayer as well as the amount of time we spend in prayer.

On the other hand, by eating prior to [the morning] prayer you will eliminate this concern. You will then be able — should you only so desire — to engage in your spiritual service in an enhanced and loftier manner.

To rectify your past conduct that was not in keeping with the above, you are to influence those around you and see to it that all those who are not healthy [and strong] — as defined in *Iggeres HaTeshuvah* cited above — should not starve themselves.

Rather, they should pray and study as souls [clothed] in a body, [thus aware of the body's needs, so] that [one's bodily requirements] will not hinder [one's spiritual] service on account of the body's hunger.

May G-d crown your efforts with success.

(*Igros Kodesh*, Vol. X, p. 326)

Nourishment Before Morning Prayers

... Picking up again on our telephone conversation:

I felt that you remained unconvinced about [the necessity to scrupulously maintain your] health in general, and in particular about having some form of pastry prior to morning prayers.

I am therefore copying here a saying of the holy Baal Shem Tov, printed in *Kesser Shem Tov* — [and] surely you are aware of what my father-in-law, the Rebbe, of blessed memory, said during his final *farbrengens*, that a chassid should study the *Kesser Shem Tov* and the *Or Torah* of the Maggid of Mezritch.

In *Kesser Shem Tov*, part I, p. 17 (in the edition that I have[5]), it states: "When a person is ill in body, his soul is weakened as well and he is unable to pray properly — this, notwithstanding the fact that he is [so sterling an individual that he is] free of sin. Therefore it is important for a person to scrupulously guard his health."

(*Igros Kodesh*, Vol. V, p. 150)

---

5.   In the *Kehot* edition, it is on p. 58.

"BETTER TO EAT IN ORDER TO PRAY
THAN PRAY IN ORDER TO EAT"

... It astounded me to learn that you conduct yourself in an undisciplined manner with regard to your eating and drinking, notwithstanding the fact that we readily observe that such conduct weakens the body and has an immediate negative impact on the study of Torah and the performance of its *mitzvos*.

It is known that my father-in-law, the Rebbe, demanded that all the *yeshivah* students conduct themselves in an organized manner regarding their eating, drinking, sleeping, etc. I trust that at least now, having received this letter, you will rectify your behavior.

There is also the well-known adage of the *Tzemach Tzedek*, "Better to eat (first) in order to [then] pray serenely than the opposite: praying in order to be able to eat."

In today's weakened generations, permission is given even to eat baked products before prayers (understandably, following the recitation of *Kerias Shema Ketanah*) to those who conclude their prayers quite a while after they rise in the morning.

One should not act stringently regarding the above [and refrain from eating,] as doing so is a stringency that leads to laxity in Divine service, [since it would then be nearly impossible to pray, etc., with the proper intent]. ...

(*Igros Kodesh*, Vol. XIV, p. 20)

COMBAT DIZZINESS BY EATING SOMETHING
PRIOR TO MORNING PRAYERS

I was happy to receive regards from you through ... . However, it upset me to hear that for the time being you are still suffering from dizziness.

You should — if you are yet not doing so— eat some form of pastry prior to morning prayers, in addition to having something to drink.

There is the known adage of the *Tzemach Tzedek* that "Better to eat in order to pray (i.e., that afterwards one can pray serenely), than pray in order to eat," (for then the person's nerves are weakened and he cannot pray with serenity; additionally, the evil inclination and the body will then be craving food with great impatience).

Many of *Anash*, our chassidic brotherhood, received a directive from my father-in-law, the Rebbe, that for reasons of health they should eat prior to the morning prayers and not suffice merely with drinking. When you conduct yourself in this manner, it will be beneficial both to your health as well as to your business.

(Igros Kodesh, Vol. VI, p. 142)

SELF-MORTIFICATION
ANTITHETICAL TO TRUE SPIRITUAL SERVICE

It alarmed me to hear that you engage in frequent fasts, that you torment yourself by not eating for many, many hours prior to prayer, and that you behave in this [tormenting] manner in other matters as well.

I am absolutely certain that this [type of behavior] leads to a deterioration of health — the antitheses of the ruling of the *Rambam* in *Hilchos Deos* beginning of ch. 4, that "maintaining a healthy and whole body is an integral part of Divine service."

It is also known that the Baal Shem Tov wrote to his disciple, the *Baal Toldos Yaakov Yosef*, that he was extremely upset to hear that he engaged in frequent fasts, etc. If this was true regarding such a giant as the *Baal Toldos Yaakov Yosef*, how much more so does it apply to people like us.

This is in keeping with the ruling of the Alter Rebbe in *Iggeres HaTeshuvah*, ch. 3: "All this applies to the strong and robust, whose physical health would not be harmed at all by repeated fasts, as in the generations of yore. But whoever would be affected by many fasts, and might thereby suffer illness or pain, G-d forbid, as in contemporary generations, is forbidden to undertake numerous fasts."

Accordingly, if you are willing to listen to me, you will immediately cease acting in this manner, and if you have taken upon yourself the above as a "*hanhagah tovah*," a "good custom," [i.e., as a proper form of conduct, undertaking to regularly act in this manner,] and you have conducted yourself thus [at least] three times, then you should perform *Hataras Nedarim*, the "Annulment of Vows."

You should eat — even cake — prior to your morning prayers. If your health demands that you eat even more, then do so. Do not rely on your own opinion on this matter, [i.e., whether you need to eat more], rather, ask the opinion of the spiritual mentor, the esteemed and revered chassid, Rabbi Shlomo Chayim Kesselman.

... I sincerely hope that by return mail you immediately set my mind at ease by notifying me that you have forsaken the path of fasting and self-mortification, and [your spiritual service] will fulfill the commentary of the Baal Shem Tov quoted in *HaYom Yom*[6] on the verse:[7] "When you see the donkey of your enemy lying under its burden ... you must come to its aid."[8]

(*Igros Kodesh*, Vol. IV, p. 430)

---

6.   Entry for Shvat 28.
7.   *Shemos* 23:5.
8.   The Baal Shem Tov explains that "donkey" — in Hebrew, *chamor*, from the root *chomer* (materialism) — refers to a person's physical body. "You must come to its aid" means that one may not rely on fasts and mortifications to break down the body's crude materialism, but must "come to its aid," by purifying, refining and elevating the body.

Change Resolution to Fast
To Resolution to Serve G-d With Joy

... With regard to fasting:

I have already told you — based on the words of the Alter Rebbe[9] — that it is not advisable to take upon yourself extra fasts in addition to those that are already on the calendar.

One of the reasons offered by the Alter Rebbe is that today's generations are weaker than previous generations and are no longer physically capable of enduring extra fasts. Obviously, my suggestion to you is therefore valid even now [that you are feeling better].

Your impending resolution to undertake fasts should be changed to resolving to serve G-d with extra measures of joy. Moreover, you should endeavor to inspire others to serve G-d in this [positive] manner as well.

(From a letter of the Rebbe, dated the 15th of Iyar, 5724)

Alternative Forms of Fasting

I was astonished to learn of your custom to fast from time to time on Mondays and Thursdays and also *erev Rosh Chodesh*. Moreover, you do so despite the known directive of the Baal Shem Tov that one should make sure to be healthy so that [ill health] not be a hindrance to the command of serving G-d with joy, for we readily observe that in this generation frequent fasting weakens one's health and hinders the performance of *mitzvos*.

Understandably, the above refers to those fasts that the person accepts upon himself (and not those fasts that are commanded by Jewish law).

Should you insist on a form of fasting, then there is the known directive of the Rebbe Maharash that this can be

---

9.   Quoted above in the text.

accomplished by refraining from unnecessary speech, even when one greatly desires to do so. This applies not only to forbidden slanderous speech, but even refraining from speaking extraneous words.

As to food fasts — this can also be accomplished by eating nourishing foods, but not seeking out those foods that are particularly tasty. ...

(Igros Kodesh, Vol. XV, p. 177)

FASTING THROUGH HOLDING ONE'S TONGUE

With regard to your fasting — I have not heard of such a path [of Divine service for today's generations]. (Understandably, this excludes those fasts that are commanded by Jewish law, and even then, only if the doctor tells you that there is no danger in your fasting.)

It is better to replace this form of fasting with refraining [and "fasting"] from doing other things that you desire, such as refraining from speaking extraneous words and certainly refraining from speaking in a slanderous manner about someone, and the like.

This [form of fasting] exhausts the evil inclination more than an actual fast, and moreover, it doesn't harm the person's health. As a result, the individual has more strength to perform *mitzvos* in general, and deeds of righteousness and kindness (*tzedakah v'chessed*) in particular.

(Igros Kodesh, Vol. XI, p. 379)

THE CHASSIDIC PATH
NEGATES FASTING AND SELF-MORTIFICATION

In your letter you write about your daily schedule, your Torah study, and prayer. I was astounded to read about your conduct with regard to your fasting.

This is truly astonishing, since — as you write in your letter — you meet with *Anash* from time to time, and still — it would seem — you are unaware that this [path of fasting] is not the spiritual pathway of the Baal Shem Tov, his disciples and their disciples, and all who follow in their footsteps.

It is true that this path [of fasting] is also one through which a person can ascend spiritually, but in addition to the fact that this is an elongated path, it also does not wholly refine the individual, and one's spiritual service is not enhanced in its entirety as it would be when one serves G-d out of joy.

This is in keeping with the verse:[10] "Serve G-d with joy." There is also the commentary of the Baal Shem Tov (quoted in *HaYom Yom*, entry for Shvat 28) on the verse:[11] "When you see the donkey [of your enemy lying under its burden] you will [be tempted to] refrain from helping it; [but] you must come to its aid."

[Says the Baal Shem Tov:] "When you see a *chamor*, a donkey — that is, when you carefully examine your *chomer*, [materiality,] your body — you will see that it is 'your enemy,' i.e., that your *chomer* despises your Divine soul that longs for G-dliness and the spiritual. Furthermore, you will see that it is 'lying under its burden' placed upon it by G-d, namely that it should become refined through Torah and *mitzvos*; but the body is too lazy to act thus.

"It may then occur to you that 'you will refrain from helping it' to fulfill its mission, but will instead follow the path of mortification of the flesh to break down the body's crass materiality. However, the light of Torah will not reside [within the individual] through this approach. Rather, 'you must *aid* it' — purify the body, refine it, but do not break it by mortification."

---

10. *Tehillim* 100:2.
11. *Shemos* 23:5.

This is particularly true in our generation when our health and strength is not as great as it used to be, and it is explained in many *sefarim* — including the *Rambam* — that when the body is weakened, it also weakens the person's intellectual capacity, which in turn hinders the individual's Torah study and prayer.

... Rather than fasting — which diminishes your body — eat at the proper time and according to the health needs of your body, in keeping with the ruling of the *Rambam*, that "maintaining a healthy and whole body is an integral part of Divine service." Replace your fasting with exerting your body in increasing its performance of Torah and *mitzvos*. ...

(*Igros Kodesh*, Vol. VII, p. 29)

CHAPTER 3
Recuperating and Convalescing

CONVALESCING

... My intent is not to lecture — rather, my intent is that the [previously mentioned] words have a practical effect:

Now that you [are out of the hospital and] back home, and not under the constant supervision of doctors, [you must see to it that you] don't overly exert and strain yourself. On the contrary, follow the instructions of the doctors and seek to be physically healthy — and thereby you will be spiritually healthy as well. ...

(Igros Kodesh, Vol. VI, p. 245)

NECESSITY OF SPIRITUAL FARSIGHTEDNESS
IN THE HEALING PROCESS

It pained me to hear that you have not been feeling well lately, and moreover, that you have not been careful in following the doctor's instructions.

I heard many times from my father-in-law, the Rebbe, the statement of his father, the Rebbe [Rashab] *Nishmaso Eden*:

"See how precious the body of a Jew is [to G-d] — for its sake has [G-d] poured forth so much [Torah and *mitzvos*]." For as is known, Torah and *mitzvos* were specifically given to souls clothed in physical bodies and not to angels.

Since the body is so precious to G-d, it follows that we are to be scrupulous in guarding [the health of our body,] which G-d placed in our trust.[1]

Our Sages have informed us (*Berachos* 60a) that "Permission was granted the healer to heal." Consequently, a doctor acts with the Torah's permission and [moreover,] in accordance with its command ["and he shall heal"].[2]

Thus, most assuredly, even if — by following the doctor's orders — one must temporarily forgo the fulfillment of a "good custom" or the observance of a *mitzvah* in the most scrupulous and beautiful manner, and so on, the Torah will amply compensate him (*"vet di Torah nit bleiban kein baal choiv"*) [for following the doctor's orders].

Forgoing for a short while, [i.e., until you feel better,] a "good custom" or observance of a *mitzvah* in the most scrupulous and beautiful manner will result in your being able to strengthen your observance of Torah and *mitzvos* many more times so, for many long and good years.

(*Igros Kodesh*, Vol. III, p. 297)

"UNPRODUCTIVE" HEALING TIME
ULTIMATELY RESULTS IN MUCH MORE PRODUCTIVE TIME

I was notified about the status of your health, and I hope that you are experiencing a daily improvement.

To someone like you I certainly don't need to emphasize that our holy Torah, the Torah of Life, provides the physician with permission to heal — from which we understand that we are obligated to fulfill the instructions of the doctor.

---

1. Strictly speaking, our bodies do not belong to us. Rather, they are G-d's property, which He entrusted to us. See *Shulchan Aruch Rabbeinu HaZakein, Hilchos Nizkei Guf v'Nefesh*, para. 4.
2. *Shemos* 21:19.

Although the thought does creep in at times that one is wasting time with matters of healing and resting and the like; nevertheless, even a small degree of reflection — in light of the above saying of our Sages [about a doctor being given permission to heal] — leads to the understanding that [the healing process] is not a waste [of time].

On the contrary — the small amount of time (that the person thinks is being) wasted results in a profit of much time in the future, time that can be utilized by the person in the service of G-d "in all his ways" — in keeping with the directive of our Sages, as explained at length in *Toras HaChassidus* — with joy and gladness of heart.

With blessings for a speedy recovery and that you may be able to convey glad tidings regarding all the above.

(*Igros Kodesh*, Vol. XV, p. 75)

SOMETIMES REDUCING STUDY TIME FOR HEALTH REASONS IS THE BEST SPIRITUAL COURSE

... In general, it is a sound suggestion that the particular individual [about whose ill health you are writing], should, at least temporarily, reduce his study-time and occupy himself with physical labor or with office work.

If, as you indicate in your letter to me, he continues to refuse to do so, [i.e., he insists on spending all his time studying,] then he should be led to understand that at times one best serves G-d by refraining from Torah study ["*Eis la'asos laHashem*" is through "*heifeiru Torasecha*"].

This is stated as well by the Great Teacher, [*HaMoreh HaGadol*] the *Rambam*, in *Hilchos Deos*, at the conclusion of ch. 3 and the beginning of ch. 4.

(*Igros Kodesh*, Vol. XVII, p. 56)

TRAVEL TO A HEALTH SPA

You write to me about traveling to Tiberius [for reasons of health] and enumerate the pros and cons:

You will pardon me, but [your reasons for not doing so] are similar to a merchant who hesitates to open a store since it would entail a monetary investment — renting a place of business, purchasing merchandise, etc.

However, by not investing, the person denies himself the opportunity to recoup his investment one-hundred fold; in this world nothing can bring benefit without first investing spiritual or physical effort or money. Once the investment is made, however, the return on the investment is manifold.

The same is true with regard to your journey: namely that the unpleasantness associated with your trip to the Hot Springs of Tiberius pales in comparison to your ability to benefit so many more times over [in terms of improved health] for many good and long days and years, benefits that will result from your taking this trip.

If only you would have traveled there last year... but one does not remonstrate about the past.

I mention this only to prove that such a journey is not only permissible and far outweighs any of the negative aspects that you mention, but is also highly desirable — even benefiting [in the long run] those who might temporarily suffer from your undertaking this journey.

With blessings, and hoping to hear glad tidings from you, and to a healthy winter in all aspects. ...

(*Igros Kodesh*, Vol. XVI, p. 213)

TRAVEL TO THE SEASHORE

In reply to your letter of the 11th of Menachem Av in which you write about the state of your health and that the doctor told you to spend some time at the seashore:

It is proper for you to do so, particularly as "the Torah has granted permission for the healer to heal," [and if he instructs you to do so, you are to obey his instructions].

Understandably, you should do this joyfully and gladly, particularly in light of the verse:[3] "Man's steps are established by G-d," and the explanation offered by my father-in-law, the Rebbe, that individual Divine providence leads man [to a particular place for a specific purpose].[4]

... This joy will assist you in improving your health, as well as in fulfilling your spiritual mission [of purifying and improving something specific] in that location.

I surely need not emphasize to you again that your mission there should be fulfilled in keeping with the doctor's instructions, i.e., without harming your physical health in the slightest.

Since both matters, [fulfilling your spiritual mission in that location and improving your health,] are *mitzvos* (since "Maintaining a healthy and whole body is an integral part of Divine service"), you will surely be able to do both. Moreover, one will assist in the performance of the other, inasmuch as "One *mitzvah* brings about another."[5] ...

(Igros Kodesh, Vol. XVII, p. 305)

"THE LOSS IS MADE UP BY THE GAIN"

This is in reply to your letter in which you describe your health situation, particularly your hoarseness:

You [write that you] have consulted with physicians and they could not find a specific cause [for your hoarseness], but they have ordered rest, at least that you rest your vocal chords by keeping your speech to a minimum. You then go on to describe in

---

3.   *Tehillim* 37:23.
4.   See *HaYom Yom*, entry for 3 Elul.
5.   *Avos* 4:2.

detail how difficult it is for you to observe [this directive] in light of your work and position.

With regard to such behavior [of following the doctor's orders], one may well say — along the lines of the saying of our Sages — "The loss is made up by the gain."[6] That is to say that what may seem to be a temporary loss [in your ability to fully do your job] will be more than made up by the ensuing gains [that will result] from resting your vocal chords. ...

(Igros Kodesh, Vol. XVIII, p. 189)

ONE MITZVAH CANNOT POSSIBLY CONFLICT WITH ANOTHER

... With regard to your health:

In general, you should conduct yourself according to the instructions of your doctor. Surely you can arrange things so that [following the doctor's instructions] will not interfere with your sacred work (avodaso bakodesh).

This is particularly so since even a person's health, that of "maintaining a healthy and whole body," is itself "an integral part of Divine service." It is thus impossible for one mitzvah, [i.e., maintaining your health,] to conflict with another: [your sacred work].

This is especially the case when one [follows the doctor's instructions] with joy, for this joy breaks and removes all physical barriers. When this occurs, the physical is not too distant from the spiritual, [and your spiritual work and physical health will coalesce]. ...

(Igros Kodesh, Vol. IX, p. 27)

---

6.   Ibid. 5:11.

"NULLIFICATION" LEADS TO GAIN

... I strongly hope that upon receiving this letter, you will immediately notify me of good news — that at least from now on you will not interfere with the doctor's instructions, but will properly follow them.

This is especially so as we readily observe that this "nullification of Torah" (*bitulah shel Torah*) — if indeed this [conduct, i.e., learning less Torah in order to follow the doctor's orders] can possibly be considered "nullification" — will soon lead to great profit.

After some time has passed, you will see that [following the doctor's instructions] will definitely hasten one's healing, until a complete degree of healing is achieved. At that time you will be able to more than make up the lost time from your Torah study.

This healing will, of course, be impossible to achieve if you do not strictly follow the doctor's instructions.

(*Igros Kodesh*, Vol. XVIII, p. 72)

"CELEBRATORY MEAL" FOR HEALING AND RECOVERY

It pleased me to be notified about your gathering together for a "celebratory meal" [to offer thanks and praise to G-d for the recovery of ...].

Such a gathering encompasses two matters of great import: [The first:] "Love your fellow as yourself,"[7] which is, "a primary principle in the Torah."[8]

[The second:] "Give thanks to the L-rd for He is good, for His kindness is everlasting";[9] "Let him give thanks to the L-rd, and [proclaim] His wonders to the children of man."[10]

---

7. *Vayikra* 19:18.
8. *Yerushalmi, Nedarim* 9:4.
9. *Tehillim* 101:1.
10. *Ibid.*: 8.

This underscores the principle of G-d's creation of the world, for which reason [when He so desires] He is capable of disrupting the natural system and order of events — performing wonders [and miraculously bringing about healing, in order] to benefit man in this physical world.

In accordance with the ruling and directive of the Alter Rebbe that the offering of thanks [for healing] represents and substantiates the individual's return to full good health (*Seder Birchas HaNehenin* 13:5, based on the words of our earlier Sages, of blessed memory[11]), may this "celebratory meal" result in your total recovery, so that you return to your former strength in literally all aspects.

G-d will surely reward all of you [attending this "celebratory meal"] with His form of remuneration, which is "measure for measure, but many times more so," that all of you be subject to G-d's form of healing, which is in a manner of "the malady shall never come to pass" in the first place, unlike man's form of healing, [which only comes about after illness has struck,] as explained by our Sages, of blessed memory. ...

(Igros Kodesh, Vol. XVIII, p. 241)

---

11. See *Ateres Zahav* on *Shulchan Aruch Orach Chayim*, chapter 219, quoting the *Mechilta* and *Rashi, et al.*

CHAPTER 4

Obeying
Doctor's Instructions

OBEY THE DOCTOR, FOR "A SMALL HOLE IN THE BODY CAUSES A LARGE HOLE IN THE SOUL"

It pleased me to receive your letter of the 24th of Cheshvan in which you notify me of the doctor's report regarding an improvement in the state of your health. May G-d will it that your health continue to improve, and like our *Rebbeim-Nesiim* were accustomed to say: "[May it go] from good to even better."

Understandably, I object to your not meticulously obeying the doctor's orders, as "Permission was granted the healer to heal."[1]

By granting this permission, healing becomes a *mitzvah* on the part of the healer,[2] as well as a notable and great *mitzvah* on the part of the individual being healed, [i.e.,] "You shall scrupulously guard your health";[3] "It is part of the service of G-d to insure that one's body is healthy and whole."[4]

Moreover, there is the caution of *HaRav HaMaggid* [of Mezritch] to his son, the *"Malach"*: "A small hole in the body causes a large hole in the soul."[5]

There are also many other similar expressions and imperatives regarding the importance of maintaining good health. However, I

---

1. *Berachos* 60a.
2. See *Taz, Yoreh Deah*, beginning of ch. 237.
3. *Devarim* 4:15.
4. *Rambam*, beginning of ch. 4 of *Hilchos Deos*.
5. *HaTamim*, Vol. VII, p. 29.

surely don't need to go on at length about something so simple and clear-cut.

... This healing will, of course, be impossible to achieve if you do not strictly follow the doctor's instructions.

(Igros Kodesh, Vol. XVIII, p. 72)

FOLLOWING DOCTOR'S ORDERS: A COMMAND OF TORAH ORIGIN

I was happy to be notified that the doctor has permitted you to return home. May G-d will it that your health continues to improve.

Surely I need not remind you that the Torah granted "permission to the healer to heal," and thus this directive is of Torah [and not Rabbinic] origin.

It is not similar to those who mistakenly say that if someone is G-d-fearing, he need not listen to the instructions of a doctor [— when the doctor's instructions seem to interfere somewhat with his religious conduct—] and may act as he understands. Indeed, the opposite is the case.

There is also the well-known aphorism of the Rebbe Rashab, who — pointing at his holy hand — said to his son, my father-in-law, the Rebbe: "See how precious [is the body of a Jew] — for its sake has [G-d] poured forth so much [Torah and *mitzvos*]." There is also the well-known saying of the Alter Rebbe:[6] "We have absolutely no conception of how precious a Jew's body is to G-d."

May G-d grant you success and may He speed your recuperation, [which will come about] through your conducting yourself according to the instructions of the doctor, the emissary of G-d, the "Healer of all flesh and Performer of wonders."[7]

(Igros Kodesh, Vol. X, p. 200)

6.　Quoted in *HaYom Yom,* entry for *erev* Rosh HaShanah.

7.　From the text of the *"Asher Yatzar"* blessing, from *Berachos* 60b.

"G-D FORBID" NOT TO OBEY THE DOCTOR'S INSTRUCTIONS

I have received a report that allegedly you are not — G-d forbid — obeying the doctor's instructions.

If this report is true, [that you are indeed not obeying the doctor,] then you will surely begin obeying him properly and will do so at the earliest opportunity, particularly as this is an explicit law in *Shulchan Aruch* — and may you convey glad tidings.

I will mention you in prayer at the holy resting place of my father-in-law, the Rebbe, of blessed memory, for good health.

(From a response of the Rebbe in 5732)

THE PHYSICIAN'S DIVINE EMPOWERMENT TO HEAL

I have been informed that your health is not what it should be and that you are entering the hospital — may it be in a good and auspicious time.

Surely you will follow the instructions of the specialists. There is the known ruling and comment of our Sages, of blessed memory, that "Permission was granted the healer to heal,"[8] meaning that the Torah not only grants permission, but also empowers [the healer to succeed in his healing].

For when G-d grants someone permission to fulfill a good and useful function, G-d also — since He is the "Essence of Goodness" — surely desires that that individual will successfully fulfill this task, and He therefore provides him with both the ability and strength to do so.

(Likkutei Sichos, Vol. XXXVI, p. 296[9])

---

8.   *Berachos* 60a.
9.   From a letter of the Rebbe, dated 13 Menachem Av, 5714.

HEALING IS FROM G-D
THROUGH THE MEDIUM OF HEALERS AND MEDICATION

In response to your letter which I received in a timely fashion:

Be assured that the blessings you received from my father-in-law, the Rebbe, will be fulfilled in their entirety.

You write that you went to a doctor; surely you are obeying his instructions.

Healing and strength both emanate from G-d. However, the Torah informs us that G-d desires that healing should come about through an agent — through a physician and through the medication he prescribes.

You should also remember always that the *mitzvos* and good deeds that G-d commanded us all to fulfill are the true healing and medication; it is they which provide health and strength, in keeping with the Rebbe's blessings to you, and the blessings of a holy individual, a *tzaddik*, will surely come to fruition.

(*Igros Kodesh*, Vol. III, p. 298)

DOCTOR'S ORDERS ARE TO BE FOLLOWED WITH THE JOY
OF BEING ABLE TO FULFILL G-D'S COMMAND

It has been some time since I received a letter from you. I hope to G-d that this is a sign that everything is well. Nevertheless, it would be appropriate for you to expressly write [to me] about this.

During these days of Kislev, the "Month of Liberation," you should act in accordance with the statement of our Sages, of blessed memory, who commanded us to follow doctor's orders and do so with a sense of joy.

It should make no difference to you in what manner and through which means you fulfill G-d's will — what is of primary importance is that you do so without reservation. Thus, when G-d commands you to obey the doctor, you should do so and be satisfied at the opportunity presented to you to fulfill G-d's will.

Consequently, you should do so with a sense of joy. And when you will act in this manner, G-d will assist you to see with your own eyes that there is indeed much to be satisfied about.

(Igros Kodesh, Vol. VIII, p. 39)

IMPORTANCE OF FOLLOWING DOCTOR'S ADVICE

... A patient may well have his doubts about the efficacy of a drug prescribed by his physician. Will he refuse to take it until he has been able to attend medical school and learn all that his doctor has learned during his lifetime of study and experience? Will he not rely on the authority of the medical specialist?

If he has doubts about the expertise of one doctor, he can obtain a second opinion, and a third; but when all agree that he needs a particular medicine or a prescribed regimen, would he refuse to take that expert advice even if he still has "strong doubts" about it?

(From a letter of the Rebbe)

USE NATURAL CHANNELS — SEEK THE ADVICE OF A PHYSICIAN

In reply to your letter ... in which you state your heartfelt desire to be blessed with additional healthy and viable children — in addition to your daughter *shetlita*. You also write that your husband does not want to ask a doctor why several years have gone by without your having children:

It is well known that although G-d is the Creator and Conductor of the world, "Healer of all flesh and Performer of wonders," the Torah demands that we also do what we can via natural channels — in the words of our Sages: "Permission was granted the healer to heal."

You should therefore speak to your husband *sheyichye* again [and try to convince him] that both you and he should visit a fertility specialist and follow his advice.

(*Igros Kodesh*, Vol. XIV, p. 383)

OBEYING THE DOCTOR — G-D'S CONDUIT FOR HEALING

... Thank you for informing me about the good news regarding your health. No doubt you are obeying the Torah directive which informs us that "Permission was granted a healer to heal,"[10] meaning that [not only does Torah grant permission, but] it also empowers the healer to succeed in his healing.

In fact, the doctor serves merely as a channel through which we receive the power and additional strength to be able to "maintain a healthy and robust body — an integral part of Divine service"— as explained by the *Rambam* in *Hilchos Deos* beginning of ch. 4, and in many chassidic discourses.

(*Igros Kodesh*, Vol. XV, p. 131)

FOLLOWING THE INSTRUCTIONS OF THE DOCTOR'S DISPATCHER

... Regarding the instructions of the doctors:

All Jews are enjoined to conduct themselves according to the Torah's directives. Since our Sages, of blessed memory, inform us that "Permission was granted to a healer to heal," this clearly indicates that a doctor is an agent [of G-d to heal].

Even though the agent may not always know the inner intent [of his Sender,] nevertheless, that which the agent states with regard to how a patient is to conduct himself emanates from the Sender. This, then, is a Torah matter.

We understand from the above that even when one does not completely understand the emissary, or even has questions about

---

10. *Berachos* 60a.

him — similar to that which you write in your letter — this should not affect his obeying the doctor's instructions.

I am therefore confident that as soon as you receive this letter, you will begin obeying the doctor's instructions. May G-d grant that your obeying and acting according to the doctor's directives be met with tremendous success in all aspects.

It is also self-understood that the conduct of not eating at the proper times, eating but once a day and the like, is completely contrary to the path of the Baal Shem Tov and of our Rebbeim and *Nesiim* who instruct us that our Divine service is to be in a manner of "you must come to its aid," i.e., to serve G-d with one's body, but not with fasts and mortifications.

I hope to receive a speedy response from you in which you notify me that you are complying with the above. May G-d grant that your actions meet with success.

(*Igros Kodesh*, Vol. XIV, p. 505)

FOLLOW THE DOCTOR'S INSTRUCTIONS — BUT DO NOT WORRY

... With regard to your question about your health:

[You should] completely cease thinking [and worrying] about it. Rather, go to a doctor and make sure to follow his instructions exactly regarding your daily schedule, etc. Do all the above but without involving your thought process, [i.e., worrying about the results and your general health]. ...

(*Igros Kodesh*, Vol. XIII, p. 308)

FOLLOWING A PSYCHIATRIST'S ADVICE

Your letter of ... reached me this morning. Though it is *erev Shabbos* — *erev* Purim, I hasten my reply because of the subject matter, especially as it also involves a mother's concern for her daughter.

To begin with the essential point: my answer to your daughter's question was that she should follow the psychiatrist's advice. It was not, G-d forbid, an attempt at evasion. It was based on common sense, since the psychiatrist is, in my opinion, the only qualified person to give advice, given his knowledge and experience.

My answer was based on the directives of the Torah that one should be aware of one's responsibility to give the proper advice after due deliberation of all the factors involved.

In light of the above:

1. Insofar as I know your daughter from her correspondence as well as from her husband, it is my opinion that the solution you presently suggest (a) will certainly cause shock and trauma, probably accompanied by feelings of guilt on the part of your daughter; (b) [and] as to how long this traumatic state would last — this would be difficult to assess, even for a psychiatrist.

2. I am surprised to note from your letter that [you believe that] your daughter knew nothing about the health of her husband. I beg to differ, for I have reason to believe that although she may not have been aware of all the specific details, she was aware that he had a health problem, etc.

3. No doubt you know, and certainly doctors know, that the health condition in question affects people in different ways: With a great many people it is a temporary [condition]. In the case of many others, it takes the form of "highs and lows," with wide-ranging variables regarding the duration of the "lows."

4. From what your daughter has written to me — although I am not at liberty to divulge anything of a confidential nature — I can say this much, that she "still" has good feelings towards her husband, and moreover, still loves him.

Therefore, even assuming that her traumatic state and guilt feelings would eventually be overcome..., it is very likely that when she hears that her husband has recovered, or, at any rate, that the "low" state improved substantially, it would reawaken her guilt feelings with all its untoward consequences.

All the above takes on even greater gravity in view of the fact that your daughter is presently carrying her husband's child, which, of course, adds an additional factor to the entire situation.

5. Much more can be said in regard to the whole situation, but I trust the above will suffice to help you understand why I cannot undertake the responsibility of advising her to pursue the solution that you suggest in your letter.

It also explains why I think a psychiatrist is the only suitable person to assess the situation and to recommend the most advisable course of action, as he is best able to take into consideration all the factors.

(From a letter of the Rebbe)

CHIZKIYAHU'S HIDING THE "BOOK OF CURES"

... It is known that regarding the *Talmudic* statement, "Chizkiyahu hid the Book of Cures,"[11] the *Rambam* has already [explained and] forewarned that this should not be understood as a condemnation of the medical arts, but that the "Book of Cures" contained *segulos* [consisting of forms of healing based on astrological charts].[12]

Truly, "Permission was granted the healer to heal,"[13] (and according to *Chassidus*, [this verse not only grants permission, but] also empowers the healer to succeed in his healing).

---

11. *Berachos* 10b; *Pesachim* 56a.
12. *Rambam's Commentary on the Mishnah, Pesachim*, conclusion of ch. 4; *Moreh Nevuchim* 3:37.
13. *Berachos* 60a.

Although the *Ibn Ezra* maintains[14] that this [permission to heal extends] only to healing the external organs and not the internal organs,[15] the widespread accepted ruling and prevailing conduct among all Jews is in accordance with the *Rambam* — that medication is used [even for healing the internal organs], as well as to have trust in G-d that He will send His "healing words" through [the channel] of "this specific doctor and this particular medication."

(Igros Kodesh, Vol. IV, p. 444)

THINK HEALTHY — BUT FOLLOW DOCTOR'S ORDERS

... I fail to understand why you are in a total panic once again with regard to your health. I have already told you and have already written to you numerous times my clear-cut and unambiguous opinion regarding this matter, [that you are in fact well].

I also stressed that in my opinion you should pay no attention to, and stop thinking about, your health situation, for you are — with G-d's help — healthy. However, concerning your actions, you are to fulfill all the instructions of the doctors.

Rather than your doing so, I observed that even when you were here you acted in an opposite manner: you delved into depressing thoughts that are entirely baseless (without any reason for doing so), and you absolutely refused to maintain a proper schedule for eating and drinking, and so on, (also without any rational reason for acting in this manner).

It seems that you continue to conduct yourself in the above manner presently as well. So what will my writing to you help, when you desire to do the very opposite [of what I tell you]?

14. *Shemos* 21:19.
15. See also *Ramban's* introduction to his commentary on the Torah, as well as his commentary on the beginning of the portion *Bechukosai*, quoted in *Taz* on *Yoreh Deah*, beginning of ch. 336.

Realize that this matter depends entirely on your desire [and decision]. ...

(Igros Kodesh, Vol. XII, p. 217)

DO NOT RUN FROM DOCTOR TO DOCTOR

With regard to the suggestion in your letter about being checked by other doctors:

After begging your pardon, I must say that ridiculous behavior must also have limits, [so stop running from doctor to doctor. Rather,] ask Dr. ..., whom you mention in your letter, to prescribe a diet of those foods and beverages that are best for you in your current state of health, approximately when you should eat during the day, how many times a day [you should eat,] and the like.

Having done so, see to it that you actually carry out his instructions!

Also cease your travels for several weeks in order to best be able to follow the doctor's instructions. If you but so desire, you will succeed in doing so.

(Likkutei Sichos, Vol. XXXVI, p. 288[16])

LEAVE THE HEALING TO THE HEALER

In reply to your letter of Thursday, *Parshas Vayechi*, in which you notify me that you have had several operations [and that you are poring over medical books], etc.:

It is regrettable that you are fixated and poring over medical books regarding that which you imagine to be your ailment. In my opinion, you should be doing only that which the Torah commands — to obey the instructions of the doctors.

---

16.   From a letter of the Rebbe, 27 Shvat, 5716.

With regard to your health, concentrate your mind and heart — i.e., your thoughts — on firm *bitachon* in G-d, Who "heals all flesh and performs wonders."

You should not dabble in medical science. This is not your province, particularly if this upsets your peace of mind and rouses within you feelings of gloom and doom. Furthermore, there is also the celebrated adage voiced by many Rebbeim of Chabad: "Think positively, and you will see positive results" ("*Tracht gut, vet zain gut*").

With regard to your healing: a) You are surely obeying doctors' orders. b) You will — as much as possible — avert your thoughts from agonizing over the state of your health. c) Be firm in your *bitachon* in G-d, for Whom there are no limitations and "who can tell Him what to do." d) Bind yourself to an even greater degree to the study of *Toras HaChassidus*. ...

(Igros Kodesh, Vol. IV, p. 130)

"DOCTOR'S ORDERS" ARE TORAH'S ORDERS

I was pleased to receive your letter in which you describe your conduct — particularly your eating habits and those matters relating to your physical health and well-being.

We are commanded in our holy Torah, the Torah [of Life, emanating] from "the Living G-d," that concerning our health we are to meticulously obey "doctor's orders," since "Permission was granted the healer to heal,"[17] and the doctor serves merely as an agent [of G-d to achieve healing].

Understandably, it is perfectly fine to voice your protests and opinions regarding the doctor's [prescribed] course of healing — including the notion you wrote to me. However, after the doctor hears you out [and then renders his final opinion], you are to

---

17. *Berachos* 60a.

follow his instructions whether you logically agree with them or not.

For, as stated above, the doctor is no more than an agent who heals at the behest and with the permission granted to him by the Torah; [and] since this [power to heal] emanates from the Torah, [the doctor's orders] are equally beneficial to body and soul.

[The above is true] even when one does not understand the [Torah's] reasoning [for following doctor's orders] or thinks differently — which in itself is also not surprising, as Torah is G-d's Divine will and wisdom, and thus it is no wonder that not everything the Torah states is comprehensible to man.

However, [it is quite clear that] man must follow all the dictates of the Torah, even when they are not understood — and understanding will eventually follow.

I trust that you will abide by all the above, and moreover do so with joy and gladness of heart.

With blessings for glad tidings regarding all the above.

(*Igros Kodesh*, Vol. XV, p. 160)

FOLLOW THE CONCURRING INSTRUCTIONS OF THE SPECIALISTS

In reply to your letter, ... in which you describe your [poor] state of health and the [negative] impact this has had on your Torah studies:

Since you are under the care of a number of specialists who are — as you write — in consultation with one another, you should follow their instructions.

May G-d will it that you see the fulfillment of the saying of our Sages: "Permission was granted the healer to heal" — and as a result, the remedy is therefore appropriate and effective.

With regard to your studies: For a certain amount of time, try to establish an easier course of Torah study (*l'girseh*) and see how that study affects you, [i.e., whether you will be able to grasp these studies].

(Igros Kodesh, Vol. XIII, p. 104)

CONTINUALLY OBEY DOCTOR'S ORDERS

... There is the known directive of our holy *Nesiim* that we are to obey the instructions of competent physicians. This [directive] applies to you as well. However, it seems that you only follow their instructions intermittently, i.e., for a lengthy period of time you stop listening to them and you conduct yourself in a manner that opposes their instructions.

The preciousness of a Jew's body has already been made clear both in the revealed and mystical portions of Torah. Accordingly, one must make an effort to keep the body healthy and well, whereby one can serve G-d without distractions [stemming from the consequences of ill health].

On the contrary, in accordance with the directive of the Baal Shem Tov,[18] [Divine service must be in a manner of]: "You shall come to its aid — [serve G-d] with the body." In present times, conducting oneself in an opposite manner is most often a result of desiring to be too clever (*veizen kuntzen*), or for even worse reasons. So abandon this path.

From now on, at least, receive from your doctor precise instructions concerning how to conduct yourself with regard to eating, drinking, etc. — and conduct yourself so. This can surely be accomplished in a manner that will not conflict — G-d forbid — with the *Shulchan Aruch*.

[When you follow the above,] this will result in rapid healing and you will return to sound health.

(Igros Kodesh, Vol. XI, p. 84)

---

18. See *HaYom Yom*, entry for Shvat 28.

FOLLOW ALL PARTICULARS OF THE DOCTOR'S INSTRUCTIONS

I was pleased to receive your letter from the eighth of Elul where you write that you are feeling much better. May G-d grant that it be totally good — not only that the doctor should think so, but you as well should actually feel that this is so.

It is self-understood that you should take the vitamins that your doctor has prescribed. Moreover, if the doctor tells you what and when you should eat and drink, you should follow that as well. For inasmuch as a Jew's body is sacred and the Torah states: "and he shall heal,"[19] the doctor is thus Torah's agent to bring about healing.

(Igros Kodesh, Vol. XI, p. 379)

EAT THE FOODS THE DOCTOR INSTRUCTS
AND A RABBI PERMITS

It is my strong hope that your health has improved.

Based on the saying of our Sages, of blessed memory, that[20] "Permission was granted the healer to heal," you are surely following the instructions of your doctors. [By this I refer] not only to the medicinal and therapeutic aspect of your healing, but also regarding [their instructions about] your diet, which also plays a part in the healing process.

Do not be overly inflexible regarding the foods you eat, for all Jews were commanded to guard their bodies and health. Thus, you should be meticulous in listening to the doctor and eating those things that according to Jewish law you are permitted to eat inasmuch as the doctor told you that you should eat them. This is particularly true in light of the saying of the Alter Rebbe:[21] "We have absolutely no conception of how precious a Jew's body is to G-d."

---

19. *Shemos* 21:19.
20. *Berachos* 60a.
21. Quoted in *HaYom Yom*, entry for *erev* Rosh HaShanah.

Therefore, those foods and liquids that the doctor tells you to consume — and a rabbi who issues *halachic* rulings permits them — you should eat and drink them accordingly. May it be "to your health!" (*zol zain tzu gezunt*) materially and spiritually.

(*Igros Kodesh*, Vol. XIII, p. 473)

HEALING WITHIN THE CONFINES OF NATURE

... No doubt your wife received instructions from the doctor and is obeying them. ... For although G-d is the "Healer of all flesh and Performer of wonders," it is still expected that something be done within the realm of nature — even if this is but very slight.

[In relation to this,] there is a story that I once heard from my father-in-law, the Rebbe, that once a very sick person came to the Alter Rebbe and he healed him with a piece of *shemurah matzah* and half a glass of water. We thus see that some basis in nature is required. May G-d hear your prayer and request, and may you be able to convey glad tidings.

(*Igros Kodesh*, Vol. IV, p. 352)

WHEN TO CONVINCE THE DOCTOR

In reply to your letter of the twenty-first of Menachem Av, in which you write that the basis and reason for not participating lately in the work of *N'shei u'Bnos Chabad* and other similar organizations is connected to the view of your doctors [who want you — for reasons of health — to ease up on your activities]:

It is understandable that doctor's orders are to be followed, as our Sages, of blessed memory, have said:[22] "Permission was granted the healer to heal."

---

22. *Berachos* 60a.

However, when you know that your work brings you in contact with others, and you also know that it benefits a particular group of people — spiritually, materially, or both — then not only will this work not weaken you, but on the contrary, it will strengthen you.

Moreover, this will not only provide you spiritual satisfaction, but will literally improve your physical health as well; physicians also recognize this and therefore advise people to remain active, each individual according to his state of health.

Taking into account the above, my opinion with regard to your question is the following:

You should take an active and diligent role in the work of *N'shei u'Bnos Chabad*, as well as activities that will benefit *Yeshivah Achei Temimim* in Tel Aviv, and other similar activities. Surely you can arrange that your work will not involve climbing stairs, since, as you write, this is difficult for you.

I believe that when you consult with the doctor whose diagnosis was more accurate than that provided by the first doctor you visited (for which reason it is advisable to follow his instructions), he will surely be in complete agreement with the above.

This is particularly so since we know that doing good things for others increases G-d's blessings regarding those matters that the person or his family needs. In addition, I surely need not draw your attention to the directive of *Toras HaChassidus* that everything should be done with joy, in which case one is more successful as well.

(*Igros Kodesh*, Vol. XIII, p. 415)

CHAPTER 5

Maintaining a Positive Spiritual Attitude When Ailing

COMPLETE FAITH AND TRUST IN G-D

I duly received the telephone message as well as the letter regarding the state of your health, and I will remember you in prayer at the holy resting place of my father-in-law, the Rebbe, of sainted memory, in accordance with your request.

It is surely unnecessary to emphasize to you the importance of *bitachon* — complete trust in G-d — not just as an abstract belief, but in a way that truly permeates one's whole being.

For, in addition to this being one of the very fundamentals of our faith and way of life, it is also a channel to receive G-d's blessings, especially for the success of your medical treatment, which has to be undertaken in the natural order, inasmuch as our holy Torah itself gives authority and power to doctors to heal and cure.

You surely also know that [living one's] daily life in accordance with the will of G-d is the channel through which Jews receive G-d's blessings in all needs, and additional efforts in this direction bring additional Divine blessings.

(From a letter of the Rebbe, dated *Rosh Chodesh* Kislev, 5733)

FAITH AND TRUST IN G-D

One of the differences between *emunah*, faith, and *bitachon*, trust, is that *emunah* is a constant factor in one's life. A believer accepts those points he believes in with absolute certainty, seeing them as givens. Therefore they are constant [factors in his life].

[This applies] even when his *emunah* involves [not only abstract principles, but] matters that [also] affect his actual [life],[1] e.g., the point under discussion, that "his provisions are granted to him by Divine providence."

It is not appropriate to say that he believes this concept only during the time that he is involved with his livelihood. On the contrary, this *emunah* is a constant.

Regarding *bitachon*, however, a person's certainty and reliance on G-d with regard to his livelihood is a feeling that is aroused when a person is in need.[2]

When a person is involved in earning his livelihood, he puts his trust in G-d, [confident that] "G-d, your L-rd, will bless you in all that you do."[3] He trusts that G-d will certainly bless his efforts; that his efforts will bear fruit.

To cite another instance: When a person finds himself in a difficult situation and does not see any natural way of being saved, he does not despair and ask:[4] "From where will my assistance come?"

Instead, he is certain [and trusts] (because of his *bitachon* in G-d) that G-d — Who is the Master of nature and can alter [the

---

1.   Similar concepts apply with regard to [another dimension of] *emunah*, that it is an encompassing power [which does not necessarily produce an internalized effect on a person. This] also [applies] even with regard to actual [life situations], and it is possible that before breaking into a house, a thief will cry out to G-d (*Berachos* 63a, according to the version of the *Ein Yaakov*). [Such a contradiction] is not possible with regard to *bitachon*.

2.   [It is true that] the concept of *bitachon* always exists within the feelings of the person who possesses *bitachon*. The actual arousal and revelation of the quality of *bitachon*, however, occurs only when [this quality is] called upon in actual life. See the beginning of *Nesiv HaBitachon* in *Nesivos Olam* by the *Maharal*.

3.   *Devarim* 15:18.

4.   *Tehillim* 121:1.

situation as He desires][5] — will certainly help him. He knows: "My assistance is from G-d, Maker of heaven and earth."[6]

Moreover, the person's *bitachon* itself serves as a medium that draws down the deliverance from G-d and the satisfaction of the person's needs, for *bitachon* means[7] that a person relies on G-d to bring him good in an open and revealed manner.

... When a person displays utter *bitachon* in G-d and has simple and absolute trust that G-d will provide him with revealed good — despite the fact that this is unattainable according to ordinary calculations and circumstances — his *bitachon* itself will serve as a medium to draw down influence from Above. ...

(*Likkutei Sichos*, Vol. XXVI, p. 96ff.)

IMPORTANCE OF BITACHON FOR GOOD HEALTH

... [It is true] medically as well, that the greater one's degree of *bitachon*, the greater one's amount of energy, and the better one's health and spirits — all this increases a person's accomplishments and success.

(*Igros Kodesh*, Vol. XVIII, p. 236)

"HEALER OF ALL FLESH AND PERFORMER OF WONDERS"

... I surely don't need to draw your attention to the fact that G-d is — as stated in the text of the morning blessings established by the Men of the Great Assembly — the "Healer of all flesh and Performer of wonders."

Since the Sages established this blessing to be recited with the inclusion of G-d's holy Name and Kingship, there is no doubt at

---

5. See [the statements of] Rabbeinu Yonah [quoted in] *Kad HaKemach, erech Bitachon*. See [also] the marginal note in *Likkutei Sichos*, Vol. III, p. 883 (also printed in *Igros Kodesh* of the Rebbe Rayatz, Vol. VI, p. 398ff.).

6. *Tehillim, loc. cit.*:2.

7. See also *Likkutei Sichos*, Vol. III, *loc. cit.*

all [that the blessing will be fulfilled,] since it is forbidden to recite a blessing [that contains G-d's holy Name and Kingship] regarding something doubtful. ...

Consequently, increasing your *bitachon* in G-d will, in and of itself, improve your health — in addition to the added measure of success of your medical treatment. The conduits and vessels through which one receives G-d's blessings are Torah and *mitzvos* in general, and their enhanced performance during times of need and difficulty in particular.

Surely you will act in this manner proportionate to your present spiritual standing — and "He who increases [his good deeds] will see a corresponding increase [of blessings]."[8] ...

You will no doubt observe the three well-known daily lessons that apply to all, as established by my father-in-law, the Rebbe, of blessed memory. They are: the daily portion of *Tehillim* — as divided by the days of the month — after your morning daily prayers; *Chumash,* the daily section of the weekly Torah portion, together with the commentary of *Rashi* — on Sunday, from the beginning of the Torah portion till *Sheni,* on Monday from *Sheni* to *Shelishi,* and so on; and *Tanya,* as divided by the days of the year. ...

(Igros Kodesh, Vol. X, p. 71)

ASSISTING OTHERS IN BITACHON
ASSISTS IN ONE'S HEALING

I received your letter of the 19th of Teves in which you write that you are in the hospital under the care and supervision of doctors. You describe the state of your health and your apprehensions.

It is known in general that each and every one of us must be firm in our *bitachon* — our faith and trust — in G-d, the "Healer

---

8.   See *Taanis* 30b and *Rashi's* commentary there.

of all flesh and Performer of wonders." The greater your degree of *bitachon* in G-d, the greater will be the improvement in your health.

However, at the same time, our holy Torah also says, "and he shall heal": that the doctor is the agent of the "Healer of all flesh" to bring about healing to the person in need of it.

In order to strengthen one's *bitachon* and increase G-d's blessings, one's performance of Torah and *mitzvos* must also be augmented, each and every individual according to his spiritual level.

Moreover, do not be content with working on yourself only, rather, encourage those who are in your locale as well — surely you can affect and encourage them to some extent — both with regard to faith and trust in G-d, as well as increasing their performance of Torah and *mitzvos*.

Since G-d conducts Himself "measure for measure, [but many more times so,"][9] by seeking to enhance the spiritual or physical health of one's fellow Jew, the A-mighty rewards this effort many more times over.

May G-d grant you success, so that you will be able to convey glad tidings regarding all the above.

(Igros Kodesh, Vol. VIII, p. 145)

GENUINE BITACHON DIRECTLY IMPACTS
A HEALTH SITUATION

In addition to the primary aspect of possessing *bitachon* — which is a fundament of our faith — strengthening your *genuine bitachon* in G-d also acts as a *direct* form of healing for the above [ailment], (something which doctors acknowledge as well).

---

9.   See *Sotah* 8b.

See to it that you observe *Chitas*, [the daily portion of *Tehillim* as divided by the days of the month, recited following morning prayers; the daily section of the weekly Torah portion; and *Tanya*, as divided by the days of the year].

I will mention you in prayer at the holy resting place of my father-in-law, the Rebbe, of blessed memory, for good health.

(From a response of the Rebbe in 5732)

BITACHON AS A CHANNEL FOR G-D'S BLESSINGS

I duly received the telephone message as well as the letter regarding your state of health, and I remembered you in prayer at the holy resting place of my father-in-law, of saintly memory, in accordance with the request.

From what I have been informed about your progress in matters of Jewish observance, it is surely unnecessary to emphasize to you the importance of *bitachon* — complete faith and trust in G-d — not just as an abstraction, but in a way that truly permeates one's entire being.

In addition to *bitachon* being one of the foundations of our faith and way of life, it is also a channel to receive G-d's blessings, especially for the success of the medical treatment, which has to be undertaken in the natural order since our holy Torah empowers and authorizes doctors to heal and cure.

You surely know, too, that living one's daily life in accordance with the will of G-d is the channel through which Jews receive G-d's blessings in all their needs; added efforts in this direction bring supplementary Divine blessings. ...

(From a letter of the Rebbe, dated *Rosh Chodesh* Kislev, 5733)

REALIZE THAT HEALTH PROBLEMS MAY BE A DIVINE TEST; WITHSTANDING THE TEST DISSOLVES THE DIFFICULTIES

... With regard to your health situation, etc.:

The purpose [of that which I mentioned above regarding individual Divine providence, etc.], is not to justify your situation, but to suggest to you that possibly the meaning of it all is that you are being subject to a test [from Above,][10] (something that comes about specifically from something problematic and incomprehensible).

Then — as is the pattern with Divine tests — when one recognizes that[11] "G-d is testing you in order to know whether you love Him with all your heart and soul" and one withstands the test, then the [troublesome] situation [and test] disappears (for it has already fulfilled its "purpose"), and the person returns to his previous strong state.

With blessings for a full and speedy recovery. ...

(*Igros Kodesh*, Vol. XXIV, p. 167)

PAY NO ATTENTION TO THE
TEMPTATIONS OF THE EVIL INCLINATION
WHICH SEEKS TO THWART YOUR BITACHON

It was reported to me that your health is not satisfactory:

At an auspicious time, I will mention you in prayer at the holy resting place of my father-in-law, the Rebbe, of blessed memory, that you be able to convey to me glad tidings regarding your health.

Knowing you and your family as a whole, I need not emphasize that I am surprised by your minimal amount of *bitachon* in G-d, Who oversees with individual Divine providence each and every one of us down to our smallest details. This is particularly so in your situation, where you have witnessed G-d's kindnesses so many times.

---

10. See *Sefer HaMaamarim Melukat*, Vol. I, p. 188ff., and sources cited there.
11. *Devarim* 13:4.

Surely this must logically lead to a strengthening of your *bitachon* in G-d and to a reduced amount of worry. This should also lead to having established times for Torah study and performing *mitzvos* with joy and gladness of heart, without paying attention to the temptations of the evil inclination which seeks to convince you otherwise — it is not for nothing that the evil inclination is described as an "old fool."

I hope that by the time you receive my letter, your health will have already improved and you will be able to convey to me glad tidings regarding all the above.

(Igros Kodesh, Vol. XXIV, p. 274)

EVEN WHEN A PATIENT IS UNDER THE DOCTOR'S CARE THE PATIENT REMAINS UNDER G-D'S CARE

In reply to your undated letter in which you write that your wife *tichye* was told by the doctor that she must go to the hospital for several days in order to take tests, but your wife is frightened and terrified of hospitals for various reasons (reasons that are absolutely groundless):

Explain to her — using the appropriate words in light of her present frame of mind — that G-d created the world and conducts the world, both that half of the globe where I find myself, as well as that half of the globe where she and you find yourselves.

[Explain to her that] "He spoke and it came to be; He commanded, and it endured"[12] — that nothing happens in the world without G-d, and whatever He desires, happens. G-d, however, wants us to make a vessel in nature, i.e., that things should happen in a natural way.

When a Jew, man or woman, does not feel well and a doctor needs to be summoned, this does not mean that the doctor will do

---

12. *Tehillim* 33:9.

whatever he desires, rather the implication is that G-d chose this doctor as His agent through whom this task [of healing] will be carried out.

When one has *bitachon* in G-d, without harboring any doubts that it is He Who conducts the world, one then merits to see with one's physical eyes [how G-d truly conducts the world] in all aspects of one's life. [For then the individual merits to see] how G-d holds on to the hand of every one of us and leads us in the best possible material and spiritual paths.

Therefore, if your wife goes to the hospital on the instructions of the doctor, she still remains under G-d's authority, and G-d will protect her and see to it that matters follow the course that is best for her, both for the health of her body as well as for the health of her spirit.

On her part, she need but be strong in her faith and trust in the blessing she received, currently receives and will continue to receive from my father-in-law, the Rebbe, הכ״מ, that she will be healed. May you and your wife speedily be able to convey the glad tidings that she has recovered and feels well.

No doubt your wife places *tzedakah* in the charity box of R. Meir Baal HaNes prior to candle lighting *erev Shabbos* and *erev Yom Tov*, and you recite daily the Rebbe's chapter of *Tehillim*, currently chapter 71, at least until the tenth of Shevat, 5711. Understandably, all the above, [the conduct of giving *tzedakah* and reciting *Tehillim*,] is to be done *bli neder*.

(Igros Kodesh, Vol. III, p. 441)

COMBINE OBEYING THE DOCTOR'S INSTRUCTIONS WITH COMPLETE BITACHON IN G-D'S HEALING POWERS

I was happy to receive your letter of the 23rd of Cheshvan in which you write that your health has improved and that the doctor is optimistic that your health will keep on improving.

I will *bli neder* fulfill your request and pray for your speedy recovery when I am at the sacred resting site of my father-in-law, the Rebbe, of blessed memory. I hope that you will be able to inform me in your next letter that you are getting better and better.

Generally, in such matters one is to obey the doctor — by avoiding climbing steps, and so on. At the same time, however, you are to be strong in your *bitachon* in G-d, "Healer of all flesh and Performer of wonders," that you will surely become well. The more powerful your *bitachon*, the quicker your healing will come about. ...

(Igros Kodesh, Vol. XXI, p. 136)

A HEALTHY DOSE OF BITACHON

From time to time I inquire about your welfare and receive news about you from .... Lately I heard from him that your frame of mind is not as it should be.

[When he informed me of this,] I was quite surprised, particularly when remembering you and knowing of your great degree of *bitachon* in G-d, [which should automatically cause you to be in a better state of mind,] for when a Jew relies on G-d, there is no room for worries and the like.

Although the Torah states that a Jew is to do whatever he can through natural means, the very same holy Torah says that his natural efforts are to go hand in hand with a strong degree of *bitachon* in G-d, Master of the world, Who takes care of each and every person — it's just that G-d desires that we do that which we should do [via natural means].

Thus, when it comes to one's health, one should visit a doctor and follow his directives; when it comes to making a living, one should seek to improve his business; and if there are problems with children, then one should seek the counsel of friends — one's good friends.

However, in conjunction with the above, one is to know and be assured that the blessing and success comes from G-d, from His "full, open, holy and generous hand."[13] Understandably, a person cannot possibly know G-d's "calendar," [i.e.,] when His blessing will arrive; however, the stronger one's *bitachon*, the earlier the arrival of the blessing.

This is particularly so in your case, where you have enlarged the "vessels" to receive G-d's blessings by strengthening your observance of Torah and *mitzvos* in your daily life, [e.g.,] *kashrus*, *tefillin*, observance of *Shabbos* and *Yom Tov,* and the like.

Additionally, you also have the merit that by your example you have affected and brought other Jews as well to conduct themselves in accordance with G-d's will and you have drawn Jewish families closer to Judaism: a truly great merit.

I therefore hope to receive cheerful news from you, that not only has your *bitachon* in G-d not diminished, but on the contrary, it has become even stronger and that in this spirit you are following the instructions of the doctor as well as the other things that are to be done via natural means. [Having done so,] I then hope and pray and am confident that you will see G-d's blessings in a revealed manner. ...

(From a letter of the Rebbe, dated *Rosh Chodesh* Sivan, 5732)

UTILIZING ONE'S FAITH AND BITACHON

In reply to your letter of *Rosh Chodesh* Iyar in which you offer a brief summary of your [difficult] life and your present [unsatisfactory] health situation:

I hope that I need not stress to you that one of the foundations of our pure faith and holy Torah — called *Toras*

---

13. From the text of the "Blessing After the Meal."

Chayim, the Torah of Life, for it is the Jew's guide to how he should conduct himself in his daily life in all aspects — is having strong *bitachon* in G-d.

As explained in numerous places in our sacred books, Divine providence extends to every single individual and to all his needs. The manner and the vessels through which one receives G-d's blessing is through having faith in Him as well as conducting oneself in accordance with our holy Torah, the Torah of Life. And "There is nothing that stands in the way of one's desire."[14]

The greater and deeper your *bitachon,* the stronger and more quickly will you receive G-d's blessing.

People generally ask, and particularly regarding the numerous matters that are incomprehensible to the human intellect, why something happened in a particular way and not in another. However, this may not, Heaven forbid, influence our connection to G-d and our *bitachon* in Him.

I get the impression from your letter that you are surely connected with a synagogue and rabbis, etc. Surely they will explain to you and make you aware of the above in greater detail. Most important, however, is your faith and resolve that since G-d is the Essence of Goodness, this goodness will eventually come to fruition and you will be able to convey glad tidings.

I would suggest that you have your *tefillin* checked, and that before putting on your *tefillin* every weekday morning you give a few cents to *tzedakah.*

(*Likkutei Sichos,* Vol. XXXIX, p. 297[15])

ANXIETY VERSUS BITACHON

As for the matter of feeling depressed, etc., [because of the state of your health], ... surely you know that one of the basic

---

14. *Zohar* II, p. 162b.
15. From a letter of the Rebbe, dated 19 Iyar 5725.

tenets of our faith and our Torah, called *Toras Emes*, the Torah of Truth, is to have complete trust (*bitachon*) in G-d, Whose benevolent Providence extends to each and everyone individually.

It is necessary to reflect on this often, for [if one does] then one can see that, being under G-d's benevolent care, there is no room for anxiety or worry. This is why the Torah is called *Toras Chayim*, the Torah of Life, for it is the Jew's guide for life and for his way of life.

And although in certain situations, [when there are health issues, etc.,] it is necessary to consult a doctor and follow his instructions since the Torah expects a Jew to do everything necessary in the natural order of things, at the same time it is necessary to have complete *bitachon* in G-d and dismiss all anxiety.

It would be well to have your *mezuzos* checked to make sure they are kosher and properly affixed. Also, you no doubt know of and observe the "good custom" — *bli neder* — of putting aside a coin for *tzedakah* before lighting the candles.

May G-d grant that you should have good news to report.

(From a letter of the Rebbe, dated the 21st of Kislev, 5733)

Bitachon in G-d, the True Healer

I received your letter in which you write about your health, etc.:

Although you do not mention it, I hope and trust that you are in consultation with a suitable doctor, while putting your complete faith in G-d, the true "Healer of all flesh Who performs wonders," while doctors are only G-d's agents. ...

(From a letter of the Rebbe in the year 5725)

FAITH IN G-D ASSISTS THE HEALING PROCESS

It shocked me to learn that you have been unwell for the last few weeks. Hopefully, by the time you receive this letter you will already be feeling better and you will be able to personally notify me [about your improved health].

[Personal notification would be better,] for with regard to all matters of Torah and *mitzvos*, [including the conveyance of tidings about improved health,] "It is a greater *mitzvah* to do something oneself than to do it through an agent;"[16] [since] "maintaining a healthy and whole body is an integral part of Divine service,"[17] [i.e., since it is a *mitzvah*, it is thus a greater *mitzvah* for you to notify me personally].

The simple faith of each and every Jew and Jewess is such that it impels them to believe that G-d alone is the Master of the entire universe and all that is found therein — and this physical world and every single man and woman are included in the above.

Since G-d is the "Essence of Goodness," He surely desires to bestow on each and every man and woman nothing but kindness and goodness — and good health is one of the fundamental expressions [of G-d's benevolence,] as explained in the *Rambam, Hilchos Deos*, the conclusion of ch. 3 and the beginning of ch. 4.

There is also the well-known commentary of the Baal Shem Tov on the verse:[18] "When you see the donkey of your enemy lying under its burden ... you must come to its aid"[19] — as explained in the discourse [*Basi leGani*] of *Yud Shevat*, 5713.

---

16. *Kiddushin* 41a.
17. *Rambam, Hilchos Deos*, beginning of ch. 4.
18. *Shemos* 23:5.
19. The Baal Shem Tov explains that "donkey" — in Hebrew, *chamor*, from the root *chomer* (materialism) — refers to a person's physical body. "You must come to its aid" thus means that one may not rely on fasts and mortifications to break

When you will (not only know, but actually) perceive and feel all the above, your soul will inevitably be suffused with an inner calm that leads to an immediate improvement in your health and a speedy recovery. ...

(Igros Kodesh, Vol. VIII, p. 262)

WHEN ONE POSSESSES A TRULY GOOD MASTER THERE IS NO ROOM FOR CONCERN

... I am surprised that you are so worried about your health, when G-d, blessed be He, says,[20] "Lift up your eyes heavenwards and see Who created all this." When one looks with open eyes at what is happening around him, he sees that G-d directs the entire world.

Any rational person must come to the conclusion that since G-d is the true and only Master of the entire universe, and He is also the Essence of Goodness, then surely everything will lead in the direction of good. When one has a good master, one need not worry at all, for there is no doubt that the master knows what is "good," and what is "even better than good."

It is also understandable that the evil inclination mixes in from time to time and confuses man's thoughts. But should one be thrown by, or believe in, that which comes from the "old and foolish king[21]"?

May G-d help that you be able to perform the directive of "Serve G-d with joy."[22] When you will do so in a truthful manner, then you will see with your very own eyes that there do indeed exist matters that you can be satisfied and joyous about.

(Igros Kodesh, Vol. IX, p. 103)

---

down the body's crude materialism, but must rather "come to its aid," by purifying, refining and elevating the body.

20. *Yeshayahu* 40:26.
21. *Koheles* 4:13.
22. *Tehillim* 100:2.

OPTIMISM AND POSITIVE THINKING ARE CALLED FOR

... You write that you are thinking of spending the upcoming days of Rosh HaShanah at home, although many of your fellow students in *Tomchei Temimim* will be spending the holiday in the environs of the *Yeshivah*. You add that you are thinking of doing so since your father's health is not at all as it should be.

I was astounded and alarmed at the extent of your lack of *bitachon* in G-d: At the conclusion of the month of Menachem Av you are confident and certain that in more than a month's time your father's health will still — G-d forbid — not be what it should be and for this reason you will minimize your service of prayer, etc., [by leaving the environs of the *Yeshivah*]!

It would have been far more appropriate and fitting for you to heed the saying of our holy Rebbeim and *Nesiim*, "Think positively and you will see positive results."[23]

You should be filled with *bitachon* that your father's health situation will surely improve, and thus you will be able to increase your spiritual service, "service of the heart" (prayer), as much as is required [by remaining in the *Yeshivah* for Rosh HaShanah].

(Igros Kodesh, Vol. IX, p. 281)

"SERVING G-D JOYFULLY" — ALL THE TIME

It pained me to hear from others far from pleasing news about your present [negative] mood and state of mind:

To someone like you, I certainly don't need expound at length about how astounding and perplexing your behavior is, particularly in light of the *Rambam's* ruling at the conclusion of *Hilchos Lulav* concerning [the vital importance of] serving G-d joyfully.

---

23. See *Sefer HaSichos 5688*, p. 4; also *Likkutei Sichos*, Vol. XXXVI p. 4, and sources cited there.

In conjunction with the above ruling, there is also the ruling of the *Rambam* as well as the *Tur* and *Shulchan Aruch, Orach Chayim*, ch. 231, that one is to serve G-d "in all your ways," i.e., twenty-four hours a day. From this we understand that one must be joyful during the entire course of the day.

This is particularly so according to that which has been expounded upon in many places in *Toras HaChassidus* — the "Luminary of Torah" — regarding the various aspects of "In all your ways you shall know Him," as well as the greatness and importance of performing a *mitzvah* with joy (see also *Torah Or*, p. 20b).

[The cause for joy is] even more relevant to you personally, and even from the point of view of your "animal soul," as you surely do not forget your health situation two or three years ago and the fright and anxiety that it caused you then.

Even if you consider this matter but briefly, you will see the individual Divine providence and kindness that G-d has showered upon you in an open and revealed manner.

Can it possibly be said then — Heaven forbid and forfend — that "G-d's hand is too short,"[24] [i.e., that He is incapable of helping you in your present situation]?

Even when drawing down and receiving G-d's Divine blessings here below, you are required to be joyful — not only an intellectual manner of joy that does not actually affect the heart, but true, unqualified and unbounded joy ("*simchah on pshetlach*").

Then [we will see] the complete fulfillment of that which is stated in the holy *Zohar* (II, p. 184b): "They — this physical world and man in general — exist by the 'radiant countenance' that comes from below. [Man's 'radiant countenance'] correspondingly draws down upon him these selfsame qualities from Above. Man's joy draws down a corresponding measure of joy from Above."

---

24. *Bamidbar* 11:23.

In addition to all the above — if indeed anything can truly be said that is more valid and convincing than the above (*keYehudah v'oid likra*):

All physicians are in agreement that a joyful and happy state of mind increases physical, mental and spiritual health and well-being, and assists the healing process.

May G-d will it that you increase your established times for Torah study in general — as the verse states: "G-d's precepts are just, gladdening the heart" — and the study of *Toras HaChassidus* in particular. Moreover, see to it that others increase their Torah studies in like manner as well.

Performing all the above will greatly enable and enhance the ability for joy to "reside in your abode," to the extent that according to Jewish law you will be able to make the blessing, "in whose abode there is joy."[25]

(*Igros Kodesh*, Vol. XIII, p. 181)

ALL IN GOOD TIME

In reply to your letter of the sixth of Iyar:

It astonishes me that you repeat your request over and over again [that you be granted an immediate full recovery,] when I have already written to you in the past that you may be fully confident in G-d "Who does everything perfectly in its proper time." This emphasizes two things: [your recovery] will be in its proper time; it will be "perfect," [i.e., you will indeed have a complete recovery].

May G-d will it that the medical procedure be successful at its appointed time, and that you will be able to convey glad tidings. ...

(*Igros Kodesh*, Vol. XVIII, p. 377)

---

25. From the introductory text of the "Blessing After the Meal" during a wedding feast or whenever the *Sheva Berachos* are recited.

FEEL CONFIDENT THAT YOU WILL SOON BE HEALED

... Rabbi ... conveyed to me that you and your wife are not feeling well:

Both of you should feel confident that you will soon begin feeling better, particularly as we are drawing close to the festival of Shavuos, "the season of the Giving of our Torah," at which time — as stated in the *Midrash* — all Jews were healed of all their ailments.

[The fact that G-d made certain that all Jews were healthy when He gave us the Torah] also serves as further proof to that which the Baal Shem Tov states in one of his discourses, that G-d desires that we serve Him *with* our bodies, [i.e., in good health]— as opposed to afflicting our bodies.

We should serve G-d with joy and in good health, devoted to the performance of Torah and *mitzvos*. ...

(Igros Kodesh, Vol. VI, p. 52)

"CEASE YOUR LAMENTS!"

After a long interruption I was happy to receive your letter, although I was not overly pleased by its content, as I see from it that you are overly concerned with the health of your children and you conclude your letter with the question, "What can I do besides cry and lament?"

The first thing for you to do is to cease your crying, etc. This is in keeping with the saying often repeated by my father-in-law, the Rebbe, in the name of Jewish greats of previous generations, that it is necessary to serve G-d with joy.

The holy *Zohar* declares that when one is joyful and strong in his *bitachon* in G-d, this also serves as a *segulah* (catalyst) for G-d to grant many more things that will serve as a cause of joy and happiness — regarding both oneself and the entire family.

This is particularly so in your case, where your children merited to study in a [chassidic] institution for which my father-in-law, the Rebbe, had *mesirus nefesh* — this itself assures that [the chassidic path of serving G-d with joy and *bitachon*] is the path that will enable your children to be happy and successful both materially and spiritually. ...

As to your question, "What can I do?" [Act in a manner] as mentioned above: Bring about joy in your home and continue your work of spreading Judaism amongst your friends. This will hasten and increase the blessings and success in your personal matters as well. ...

(Igros Kodesh, Vol. VIII, p. 280)

SO MUCH TO BE GRATEFUL FOR

It pained me to hear that your health situation is not as it should be — most importantly, that you are somewhat dejected.

I am amazed at you — and generally speaking, at all those of our generation who were protected by G-d and are the remnant "brands saved from the fire" [of the Holocaust] — that after personally witnessing such individual Divine providence, they still retain a measure of doubt.

Not that their doubt, G-d forbid, applies to their *transcendent* degree of faith, but to the feelings in their heart — [doubting] whether G-d, the "Essence of goodness" and [consequently, since] "It is in the nature of he who is good to do good," [they doubt whether He] truly orders the life of man in each and every specific detail [since this goodness is not readily apparent].

If this faith and comprehension were to permeate the person's feelings and emotions, then he surely would rejoice in his lot, and consequently his health would be as it should be. He would then increase his efforts in his service of fulfilling his life's mission in this world.

It is true that everything a person does must also be grounded in nature, as the verse states:[26] ["G-d will bless you] in all that you do," (the reason for this is explained in many places, and among them near the conclusion of *Kuntres U'Mayon*), for which reason one must follow the instructions of doctors. Nevertheless, [having followed their instructions,] one should not take the matter [of one's health] to heart at all, as is known.

If you would heed my advice, you would take a one-or-two-week vacation to soothe your state of mind and strengthen your health through rest and relaxation. Having done so, you should steadfastly resolve to serve G-d with joy. You will then be able to continue your work and public service in good health and success.

With blessings that you be able to convey glad tidings to me regarding both yourself, as well as the rest of your family. ...

(*Igros Kodesh*, Vol. IX, p. 264)

Blessings Are Only Effective
If One Does Not Counteract Them With Ingratitude

I will read the *pidyon nefesh* attached to your letter [(in which you ask for my blessing)] at the holy resting place of my father-in-law, the Rebbe, of sainted memory.

I am astonished by your [negative] attitude, as I have written to you so often about the absolute necessity of being joyful.

Nevertheless, every letter I receive from you begins and concludes with the same tired expressions, the points being that: everything is awful — your health, your wife's and your children's; you are not earning a living; you are unhappy, etc.

All this is notwithstanding the fact that you actually observed open and revealed miracles in your life. (It seems that you choose not to remember what the doctors told you at the outset of your wife's pregnancy [about the dangers, etc.,] and how the

---

26. *Devarim* 15:18.

pregnancy and birth took place, etc., [i.e., in a totally healthful manner] — completely opposite from their prognosis.)

We have already become accustomed [to people acting in a muddled and ungrateful manner] in these times of exile — times of murkiness, concealment and doubled and redoubled darkness. But even this degree of darkness must have a limit. When it comes to you, however, it seems that all the goodness showered upon you has had no effect at all.

Although this [negative outlook] is entirely of your choosing, [and what business is this of mine]; however, it still pains me to see how a Jew torments himself about matters that have absolutely no foundation, thereby ruining his health. [In addition,] it is impossible that this is not having a damaging effect on your family as well, inasmuch as you write in all your letters that you are distressed and greatly worried.

As to your asking me for my blessings and so on — it is impossible to deprive a Jew of his freedom of choice (since this freedom is rooted in the Divine soul, which is "truly a part of G-d Above" — only there does absolute freedom of choice exist, and by extension within the Jew as well).

Therefore, should you desire [and continue to choose] to obstinately act in an irrational manner, to only see in any and all circumstances nothing but negativity, then who can possibly tell you what to do [and of what benefit to you will my blessings be]?

My hope is that notwithstanding all the above, since our Sages, of blessed memory, ruled (*Bava Basra* 12b) that whoever was dealt with kindly from Above [(as you were)] will continue to be dealt with in this kindly manner for many long years; therefore you too will continue to be granted much kindness from Above.

Nevertheless, [i.e., despite your past behavior,] it is my hope that you examine [and study] again in a truly honest manner (*aliba d'nafshei*) the statement of the sacred *Zohar* (II, p. 184b) titled "*Ta chazi*" ("Come and see"), [that when man below is of a "radiant countenance" and filled with joy and gladness, he then draws down upon him the same qualities from Above].

Moreover, there is the known nuance (*diyuk*) that in the revealed portion of Torah the oft-used expression is "Come and hear" — only hearing — although the matter [heard] may well be quite comprehensible, while in the mystical portion of Torah the commonly used expression is "Come and see" — sight — which is so much more profound than hearing, although one does not always fully comprehend that which he has seen.

With my blessing that ultimately you will devote yourself to the directive of the Baal Shem Tov and the *Nesiïm* who followed him — that service of G-d is specifically to be done with a sense of joy. [And may G-d bless] you and your entire family with good health.

(Igros Kodesh, Vol. X, p. 99)

"ALL THAT G-D DOES, HE DOES FOR THE GOOD."

I was pleased to receive your regards through .... In keeping with your request, I will mention you and your entire family in prayer at the holy resting site of my father-in-law, the Rebbe, of blessed memory, for good health and sustenance.

It is surely superfluous to point out that G-d requests that we serve Him constantly throughout the year with joy, which is to say that we are to be joyful of the fact that we are children of Avraham, Yitzchak and Yaakov, and children of G-d. Consequently, we merit G-d's watchful Providence over each and every one of us individually, and at all times and in all places.

If a person were to merit the honor of being together with a king of flesh and blood in [the king's] innermost chamber, the person's joy and exultation would be tremendous. How much more so should a person rejoice and exult at one's closeness to the King of kings, as explained at length in the 36th chapter of *Tanya*.

Another thought, connected to the previous one: When one is together with the King of kings, the Holy One blessed be He, then surely, when one realizes this, there can be no thing that is not good, for no one other than G-d has any dominion in this place, [i.e., in the place where the person finds himself together with G-d].

Consequently, even if one cannot understand the inner goodness of something that has transpired, this lack of understanding is only because that individual has not pondered deeply enough yet to understand the goodness of the event. In the end, one sees how "All that G-d does, He does for the good."[27]

I hope that the above lines will suffice to arouse in you the above comprehension, and you will immediately arrive at the understanding that every Jew must be strong in his *bitachon* in G-d, and that you will attain the proper degree of *bitachon* in G-d — moreover, all Jews have this *bitachon*, at the very least, in a concealed fashion [and it needs only to be revealed].

All the above will, in turn, enable you to be truly joyful.

(*Igros Kodesh*, Vol. X, p. 389)

FULFILL YOUR TASK AND G-D WILL FULFILL HIS

... Do not obsess about your health — of course you should take care of yourself and heed your doctors' instructions, but do not obsess over it.

Rather, you should be confident that G-d, Who directs the world as a whole for the good, will also direct your personal world for the good, providing all you need in order to be able to enjoy

---

27. *Berachos* 60b.

good health. On your part, your responsibility lies in performing Torah and *mitzvos*, thereby "cleaving to the L-rd your G-d."

When you keep the above [mutual responsibilities] in mind, then you will have good health and will not be anxious and worried. You will also then have much success not only in your spiritual affairs, but also in material matters such as your business, and the like.

I hope to hear good news from you, [including the news] that you have placed the concern about your health on G-d, while you take upon yourself the concern of matters of Torah and *mitzvos*, both your own as well as of those in your locale.

I await hearing glad tidings from you and extend to you my blessings of good health, and much material and spiritual goodness.

(Igros Kodesh, Vol. V, p. 166)

RELY ON AN INFINITELY POWERFUL AND CAPABLE G-D

I am very surprised that I have not heard from you since the time that we saw each other, and it pained me to now receive news from you that your health is not as it should be. In accordance with your request, I will mention you in prayer at the sacred resting place of my father-in-law, the Rebbe, of blessed memory, for good health — both physical and spiritual.

I believe that when we conversed, the point was also made that serving G-d with joy is one of the foundations of the system of the Baal Shem Tov. Also known is the statement of the Great Teacher, our master the *Rambam*, who states that Divine service takes place not only during prayer or Torah study, but also while eating and through [the very act of] eating, while walking and through [the very act of] walking, etc.

Since G-d does not request the impossible, G-d has certainly granted every one of us the ability to serve Him in this sacred and agreeable manner of service to the fullest possible extent.

In addition to the above, also contemplate the following: Unlike the view of idolaters who maintain, "His glory is only in the heavens,"[28] since "the L-rd is high above all nations," [29] [and consequently, overseeing matters on this earth is considered a degradation, we Jews believe that] G-d oversees each and every one of us, [including overseeing us in] our ongoing daily lives and even [overseeing] those details that people call trifling and insignificant.

There is thus no room for any anxiety and concern. Indeed, this is similar to an infant whose father is close by [and as a result has not a care in the world, as he is certain that his father is infinitely powerful and capable and will see to his every need]. However, [the analogy is not quite accurate, for] in the analogy the father is all-powerful only in the child's imagination, while in the analogue the Father, our Father in Heaven, is truly infinitely powerful and capable — as is easily understood.

I await the glad tidings that you are feeling better — and in accordance with the oft-used expression of my father-in-law, the Rebbe, of blessed memory: "You should have a healthy and happy summer."

(Igros Kodesh, Vol. XI, p. 69)

BITACHON IN A TZADDIK'S BLESSINGS MAKES THE WAITING EASIER AND HASTENS THE FULFILLMENT OF THE BLESSING

I received your letter dated September 8th and I was glad to read there that you are also already noticing — as you write in

---

28. Conclusion of *Tehillim* 113:4.
29. Beginning of the above verse.

your letter — an improvement in your son's health and that he is calmer. This concurs as well with the opinion of Dr. Wilder.

As I have already once told you, since the Rebbe, my father-in-law, gave his blessing that your son will be well, then he will surely keep his word. It is only a matter of time.

Without question, the waiting [for the complete fulfillment of this blessing] is difficult, particularly for the parents of an only child.

However, being steadfast in one's *bitachon* that the blessing will be fulfilled helps in two ways: The waiting for the complete fulfillment of the blessing becomes far easier; the stronger the *bitachon*, the quicker the *tzaddik's* promise will come to fruition.

I hope that you will be strong in your *bitachon*, stronger even than you were until now. [Strengthening your *bitachon*] reinforces my assurance that your son is becoming better and better in all aspects. ...

(Igros Kodesh, Vol. IV, p. 467)

Individual Divine Providence
Extends Particularly to Health Matters

... I trust that I need not explain to you that every Jew — man and woman, young and old — should be strong in his *bitachon* in G-d, Who oversees every aspect of all our lives with individual Divine providence, particularly with regard to matters of health. This should provide you with additional strength and increased optimism that everything will surely turn out well.

Since G-d desires that we do everything we can in a natural manner, it is therefore important that you receive the advice of an expert — in your situation a doctor who specializes in nervous and mental conditions — and follow his advice.

G-d will provide His blessing for success, and much success at that. [On your part,] the more you will strengthen your *bitachon*, the more you will see the fulfillment of His blessing.

(Igros Kodesh, Vol. XX, p. 98)

DO NOT SPEAK ILL OF YOURSELF

It pleased me to receive your letter dated the 17th of Sivan. Although the content of the letter was not of the category that brings pleasure, since you lament there your ill health, nevertheless, it was pleasing to receive a letter from you after a period of silence. I hope that I will soon receive a letter from you with joyful contents regarding both your physical and spiritual well-being.

[The importance of not verbalizing or putting into writing laments about one's ill health is understood in light of] the well-known saying of my father-in-law, the Rebbe, that the prohibition against *lashon hara*, speaking ill of a fellow Jew, includes not speaking *lashon hara* about oneself as well.

Also known is the explanation of the codifiers about the difference between *lashon hara* and *motzi shem ra*, slanderous speech: *Motzi shem ra* only applies to speaking an untruth about another, while *lashon hara* applies even if one speaks the truth. Nevertheless, [even though the person speaks the truth,] our Sages say, "*Lashon hara* harms all three,"[30] [the speaker, the listener and the individual about whom the *lashon hara* is spoken].

... This, too, is the damage done by *lashon hara* even if the matter is true, for by speaking about [the faults or failings of the other or oneself, or even about one's poor health], the person reveals and brings these [faults or failings] to the fore.

When something is drawn down into the [more physical] realm of speech [from the more ethereal realm of thought], the

---

30. *Arachin* 15b.

situation is affected to a greater extent. If, however, it remains in a concealed form, the results are not so easily realized.

I hope that by the time you receive my letter, you will already have had the opportunity to bring about some positive spiritual change among some of the neighboring patients in the hospital. ...

(*Igros Kodesh*, Vol. VI, p. 140)

BITACHON THAT G-D WILL HEAL IS IMPORTANT NOT ONLY FOR ONESELF, BUT TO INFLUENCE OTHER PEOPLE AS WELL

... I see from your letter that [not only has your own health returned, but] your wife's health has improved as well. Since you see with your own eyes that G-d has healed you and that your wife's health is also improving, you are to be strong in your *bitachon* in G-d that matters will keep on improving until you will also be satisfied [from the results].

It irks and pains me to read uncalled-for expressions in your letter. Why do you do so? — particularly when this comes from a believing Jew, one who can influence others as well.

By being weak in your *bitachon* in G-d, you, first of all, negatively impact your spiritual state as well as your health. Secondly, it takes away from your desire and longing to influence others, to make them happier and in a better frame of mind.

I hope that by the time you receive this letter, your mood will have changed to the better, and you will be following the directive of our sacred Torah,[31] "Serve G-d with joy." For as explained in our holy *sefarim*, one should and can serve G-d not only through prayer and Torah, but also when one eats, drinks and the like.

One is able to accomplish this when he lives his entire life in a joyful frame of mind. When one acts in the above manner, we indeed observe that the person is healthier, in better spirits, and

---

31. *Tehillim* 100:2.

able to accomplish more both regarding himself as well as in relation to others.

(*Igros Kodesh*, Vol. VI, p. 82)

SINCE G-D SAYS CHILDREN ARE A BLESSING, JEWS ARE DESERVING OF THIS BLESSING

... Regarding that which you write: that as a result of all the above, [i.e., your wife's difficulty in conceiving,] she has become nervous, etc.:

Relay to her [the following]: G-d conducts the world in the best possible manner; it is He Who knows what is best. And He wrote in the Torah that children are a blessing — thus Jews are deserving of this.

If this blessing [for children] is sometimes delayed, then we are to know that we all have a great Rebbe, my father-in-law, the Rebbe, הכ״ימ, and he will eventually implement all the blessings he gave to all those who are bound up with him.

It is necessary, nevertheless, to maintain the bond with him. If one, however, begins having second thoughts about whether his blessing will indeed come to pass and begins becoming nervous about it, this is a sign of weakness [in this bond,] G-d forbid. Surely, if this [uncertainty about the blessing] also has an effect on one's health, then it is a definite sign that this stems simply from the evil inclination.

You and your wife must be strong in your *bitachon* in G-d and in "His servant Moshe" of our generation, my father-in-law, the Rebbe, הכ״ימ. This in itself will assist in hastening the realization of his holy blessings for viable and healthy children and all manner of goodness.

No doubt your wife gives — *bli neder* — *tzedakah* to the charity of R. Meir Baal HaNes prior to candle lighting, and you recite every day — *bli neder* — the Rebbe's chapter of *Tehillim*, ch. 71.

When your wife *tichye* will conceive in a good and auspicious hour, you will presumably not publicize this at the beginning [of the pregnancy], but you will immediately notify the Rebbe at his holy resting site.

(*Igros Kodesh*, Vol. III, p. 386)

CHAPTER 6

Maintaining a Positive Mental Attitude When Ailing

THE LIMITS OF A DOCTOR'S PROGNOSIS

With regard to a particular situation — it is impossible to know clearly and with certainty [about the eventual outcome]. Clearly, the pronouncement of the doctor that the situation is hopeless is definitely out of place.

At the very most he can say — and indeed all that a human being is capable of saying — that he does not take responsibility for the future, but [he can say] no more than that.

(*Igros Kodesh*, Vol. XX, p. 183)

A "RADIANT COUNTENANCE" FROM BELOW DRAWS DOWN THE SAME FROM ABOVE

... I believe that in the past I have already told you about the statement in the sacred *Zohar* (II, p. 184b) that when man below is of a "radiant countenance" and filled with joy and gladness, he then draws down upon himself the same qualities from Above.

This provides us with an even better understanding of the aphorism of our holy Rebbeim: "Think positively, and you will see positive results." ...

(*Igros Kodesh*, Vol. X, p. 358)

"LECHATCHILAH ARIBER"

I have just received your letter ... in which you describe your present [poor] state of health.

Surely you have heard of the saying of the Rebbe Maharash: "People say that 'when one cannot go under [an obstacle], he should go over it.' I am of the opinion, however, that from the very beginning one should 'go over,' [i.e., 'transcend the obstacle' (lechatchilah ariber)]."

Here too as well:

Although it would seem that the state of openly revealed joy should be delayed until after you are actually healed, nevertheless, in keeping with the above-mentioned saying, it is reasonable to express this [revealed degree of] joy resulting from your [eventual] healing, although the actual healing has yet to take place.

The [joy] itself will be a catalyst to hasten the matter [of your healing]. This is in keeping with the saying often heard from the Nesiim of Chabad: "Think positively, and you will see positive results." Most assuredly [this will be effective] when you transport these [joyous and positive thoughts] into joyous words and deeds. ...

(Igros Kodesh, Vol. XVI, p. 252)

"THINK POSITIVELY..." REALLY WORKS

In reply to your letter ... in which you write about your [current poor] state of health and your [negative] thoughts, etc.:

Understandably, I am astonished by your [pessimistic] attitude, for it is well known — particularly among chassidim — that our Rebbeim and Nesiim have counseled and exhorted us to "Think positively, and you will see positive results." Moreover, as is known from many tales, [thinking positively] actually brought about a positive outcome. ...

(Igros Kodesh, Vol. XVIII, p. 174)

DIAGNOSIS MAY BE ERRONEOUS —
PARTICULARLY REGARDING INTERNAL ORGANS

... We have veritably seen G-d perform miracles beyond the bounds of nature for individuals as well, [and not just for the many as your write,] particularly during the last few years.[1]

Moreover, [in addition to G-d's ability to heal you through miraculous means, you need not be despondent because of the doctor's diagnosis, for] in many, many instances, even after having concluded a battery of tests, the doctors have erred in their diagnosis, particularly when their diagnosis related to the internal organs.

All this is in addition to the fact that new medical remedies appear almost daily.

It is however of utmost necessity, indeed it is impossible for it to be otherwise, that you strengthen your connection with G-d, "Healer of all flesh and Performer of wonders"[2] — and the "verse" is to be understood in its simple context, [i.e., you are to take this literally,] that G-d performs actual miracles and wonders for individuals, the proof being that each and every one of us recites this blessing. Surely it is totally unnecessary for me to expound further on this matter at greater length.

If only in your circumstances you did not put into practice the verse, "He who acquires more knowledge [acquires more pain," then you would be so much better off]. It would be far healthier for you to realize the saying of our Sages, of blessed memory, that "[even] the person for whom G-d performs the miracle is unaware that a miracle has been performed for him."[3]

---

1. The letter was written in the year 5713.
2. Conclusion of *"Asher Yotzar"* blessing, from *Berachos* 60b.
3. *Niddah* 31a.

It is self-understood that the above in no way negates the importance of receiving the opinions of at least two specialists in this area and their views with regard to methods of treatment.

And as known the statement of the *Tzemach Tzedek*, that the Torah states, "'Permission was granted the healer to heal,'[4] but not — Heaven forbid — to bring about a crestfallen spirit [by being the bearer of disastrous news that he says *must* inevitably occur], etc." ...

(Igros Kodesh, Vol. VII, p. 282)

WHEN NOT TO LISTEN TO THE DOCTOR

This is in reply to your letter ... in which you write about what you heard from the doctor, [i.e., a negative prognosis about your wife's health] and how disheartening this was both to you and your wife *tichye*.

I am astonished, for the saying of the *Tzemach Tzedek* in commenting on the expression of our Sages that "Permission was granted the healer to heal"[5] seems to have escaped your memory.

The *Tzemach Tzedek* noted: "'He has permission to heal,' but not — Heaven forbid — to bring about a crestfallen spirit [by being the bearer of disastrous news that he says must inevitably occur], etc."

Particularly now, in our present era, when new methods of treatment and new medications are discovered daily, it flies in the face of intellect to foretell future events as your doctor did.

If only you and your wife would be strong in your *bitachon* in the Creator and Conductor of the world, Who oversees each and every person with individual Divine providence, then in the very near future it will be clearly demonstrated to you that the doctor's prognosis is false.

---

4.   *Berachos* 60a.
5.   *Ibid.*

At the same time, it is understandable that healing needs to have at least some attachment, [i.e., it also needs — at least to some degree — to go through the channels] of nature as well. You should therefore also think about adopting a vegetarian diet.

I took great pleasure in reading that your wife *tichye* spoke to a group of women and this literally had a positive effect on her health as well — yet another proof that the doctor's prognosis was wrong.

Since Jews are, after all, "the *one* nation on earth,"[6] [i.e., there is a connection and unity between everything they do,] it therefore follows that any improvement in spiritual health must as a matter of course be accompanied by an improvement in physical health.

(*Igros Kodesh*, Vol. XV, p. 187)

Obey the Doctor
But Don't Be Fazed by His Prognosis

... Regarding that which you write about the [negative] prognosis of the doctors, I am astounded that you have altered my words, causing your mood to be not as it should:

I specifically told you and also wrote to you that you should *follow the instructions* of the medical specialists; I also told you and wrote to you many times that you should *not be fazed* by their prognostications — as the *Tzemach Tzedek* noted: "'Permission was only granted the healer to heal,' but no more than that," [i.e., not to bring about a crestfallen spirit through gloomy prognoses].

In both these matters you are conducting yourself in an entirely contrary manner: You are *not* obeying the instructions of the medical experts; on the other hand, you are disturbed and discouraged by their prognosis.

---

6.   *II Shmuel* 7:23.

[As this is your manner of conduct,] what else can I do [for you] in this matter that I have not already done? After all, one may not remove from a Jewish man or woman his or her freedom of choice. ...

May G-d grant you and your spouse *sheyichyu* success in complying [with my words] regarding these two matters, so that this will immediately result in witnessing openly revealed goodness.

(Igros Kodesh, Vol. X, p. 148)

DOCTORS WERE ENTRUSTED WITH THE POWER TO HEAL — BE INATTENTIVE TO THEIR GLOOMY PROGNOSES

... With regard to the doctors' suggestion that your daughter use a wheelchair:

My opinion in these matters is that when there is the concurrence of two doctors you may rely on their advice.

May G-d grant the doctors the wisdom and insight to make the good and correct decision for your daughter *tichye*, and that they use the healing power that the Torah granted them — but on matters other than this, they are not masters. Therefore, when you hear gloomy words from a doctor, you should pay them no heed.

Realize that this is only a test from G-d, Who wants to test you and your husband, the *Rav sheyichye*, in your faith and trust in Him. The more you intensify your *bitachon* in G-d, the quicker you will see with your own eyes an improvement in your daughter's health. May G-d help you and your husband, the *Rav sheyichye*, that this come about in actuality very quickly.

(Igros Kodesh, Vol. VI, p. 116)

PERMISSION WAS GRANTED THE HEALER TO HEAL — NOT TO PREDICT A LENGTHY HEALING PROCESS

... May you very speedily convey glad tidings with regard to your personal matter, [i.e., your health,] since you have already provided a natural vessel [for your healing to come about] by visiting a doctor.

Regarding the fact that the doctor told you that the healing process would have to take a long time — this is surely not so. Known as well is the preciseness in the expression of our Sages, of blessed memory, "Permission was granted the healer to heal,"[7] but not — Heaven forbid — to predict that the healing process will be of long duration. ...

(*Igros Kodesh*, Vol. XV, p. 176)

PANICKY RUNNING TO DOCTORS

It pained me to hear about your frantic running to doctors the whole day long; moreover, doing it over something that is entirely groundless. My puzzlement extends as well to your husband, the *Rav sheyichye*: On what grounds and for what reason is the trait of alacrity (*zrizus*) being utilized not in its correct place?

While alacrity and immediacy are generally good traits, when employed because of panic, they are surely improper. Aside from this, speediness and immediacy are not always the proper course of action.

You should be filled with faith and trust in G-d, Who creates, sustains and animates the entire world, and particularly each and every individual Jew — "the people close to Him"[8] — that G-d will provide you with good health, and that together with your husband, the *Rav sheyichye*, you will raise your son *sheyichye* "to Torah, to the wedding canopy, and to good deeds."

---

7.   *Berachos* 60a.
8.   *Tehillim* 148:14.

Indeed it is necessary to make a natural vessel for all matters, i.e., to consult a doctor and follow his instructions.

However, totally engrossing yourself in this matter, as well as intensely deliberating and debating about the exact reasons for the doctors' opinions, and immersing yourself in medicine and medical matters, is not at all your area — it belongs exclusively to those who are medical professionals so that they may faithfully perform their duties in keeping with the command, "and he shall heal."[9]

With regard to other matters, however, [i.e., once you have gone to the doctor and followed his instructions, following which all other medical concerns are not within your province,] you are to use the intellect and understanding that G-d granted you either for the purpose of Torah and *mitzvos* or for permissible matters that can eventually be transformed into *mitzvah* matters.

However, worrying and being gloomy [about your health situation] does nothing but weaken your physical and spiritual health and unsettle and disturb you, [thereby keeping you] from fulfilling the mission and objective of your lives. ...

(*Igros Kodesh*, Vol. VI, p. 111)

NULLIFY ALL THOUGHTS ABOUT YOUR BEING UNHEALTHY

... In light of your request that I respond to your letter, I am doing so although I don't know what I can possibly add to that which I specifically told you when you visited me, and which I now repeat again: You are healthy, and your pessimistic thoughts [about the state of your health] are entirely without foundation.

This is particularly so since you visited the doctor and he also told you that you are well. So you see that your visit to him was of no value; it would have been better to give the money [you spent on seeing the doctor] to *tzedakah*.

9.   *Shemos* 21:19.

May G-d help you to nullify all these negatives thoughts at least from here on, and may you strengthen yourself in your joyful study of Torah and performance of *mitzvos*. ...

(*Igros Kodesh*, Vol. VIII, p. 104)

FULFILL YOUR ROLE IN LIFE — DO NOT PLAY DOCTOR

I received your letter of the 24th of Teves in which you describe your situation — that you saw the doctor's report and that this had a very strong [negative] effect on you.

You describe [what you imagine to be] your future, for which reason you recite *Tehillim* and beseech G-d [to be kind and merciful to you,] and you ask for my opinion [on the matter].

Answer:

Your recitation of *Tehillim* and beseeching G-d is surely a good thing, as G-d is the Master of the entire universe and oversees all individuals and each and every detail of their lives.

However, I disagree with that which you write: that you thought about the doctor's report and you envision a [dismal] future, for the matter [of your future] is not in your hands [at all, but in G-d's hands,] and it was not for the purpose [of gloomily pondering your future] that you were created.

Rabbi ... writes me that you are a Jew who observes Torah and *mitzvos*. Surely, then, you believe that G-d is the Master of the universe, governing the world.

We observe that even a human boss, if he is at all competent, will separate the various components of his business so that one part will not impinge on the other and each part will serve the purpose it is meant to serve.

This is only true regarding a human being who is inherently limited in all his affairs and is consequently subject to intermittent erring. Regarding G-d's mastery of affairs, however, everything that G-d brought into existence is meant to fulfill its specific purpose, mission and goal.

When someone's impulse leads him to do something other than his mission, then this contains two faults: a) since it does not comprise the individual's mission, then nothing but damage is being done; b) this takes the person away from fulfilling the mission for which he was indeed chosen.

All the above applies to your situation as well: For any number of reasons, which are surely a result of individual Divine providence, your profession is not medicine. You have, however, been raised a Jew who observes Torah and *mitzvos*.

We know two matters from the above: a) that your Divine mission in this world does not consist of practicing medicine; [and] b) that observing Torah and *mitzvos* is your goal and mission for which reason you were created. This [goal and mission] includes the *mitzvah* of "Love your fellow as yourself"[10] and "You shall surely admonish your fellow."[11]

Moreover, in commenting upon the verse, "When you see someone naked, you should clothe him,"[12] it is stated in the *sefer* of *Tanna D'vei Eliyahu*, [that this also includes the obligation that] "When you see someone naked of Torah and *mitzvos*, see that you clothe him with Torah and *mitzvos*." This then is your goal and mission in life, the purpose for which you were created.

From all the above it is understandable that when you provide prognoses and views about the science of medicine, firstly, it directs you away from fulfilling *your* mission for which you were selected. Moreover, [by interfering] in matters of your healing, you can only do — G-d forbid — harm, but surely not any good.

---

10. *Vayikra* 19:18.
11. *Ibid.*:17.
12. *Yeshayahu* 58:7.

The harm that may be brought about [by your interference] resides in the fact that your distress [stemming from what you surmised about your medical condition] can result in imagining things that will *not come to pass*. By pondering and occupying yourself with what this doctor says and what that professor may come up with, etc., you weaken your *mazal* and your *bitachon* in G-d.

If you ask my opinion, I am telling you to conduct yourself in accordance with the demands of the Torah, which states that the Torah has granted [doctors the] permission to *heal*. This is to say that the Torah [both] granted permission to turn to doctors and provided doctors with the specific permission and ability to heal and mend people.

People therefore go to doctors and then obey their instructions. [The same applies to you: Once you have gone to the doctor and followed his instructions,] there is nothing else for you to do; you are to leave the rest to the doctor.

On your part, you are to have *bitachon* in G-d that He will grant you a long life. And in accordance with the verse:[13] "The fear of G-d leads to life," the greater your *bitachon* in G-d, the less doubts you will have in this and the more you will fulfill your mission in life — as previously stated, to observe Torah and *mitzvos* and affect others in this direction as well — the longer you will live, and I mean this quite simply and straightforwardly.

Forget totally about the medical diagnosis you found in medical books because this is not your mission in life and it is totally not in your province; since it is not in your realm, your research cannot make you better and generally it only worsens — G-d forbid — the situation.

Make sure to recite the daily portion of *Tehillim* (as divided by the days of the month) after your morning prayers and study

---

13. *Mishlei* 19:23.

Chumash every day with the commentary of *Rashi*. Take part as well in public Torah lessons, at least one of which should be in the study of *Chassidus*.

It is self-understood that you are to set for yourself the goal — as the verse states and as the Baal Shem Tov demanded of chassidim — to "Serve G-d with joy"[14] — and "serve" means both when you pray and study, as well as when you eat and drink and all the other things a person does, even your sleeping, as the *Rambam* states in *Hilchos Deos*.

When you will do this, you will begin feeling better and better, and you will become healthier and healthier and will be able to convey glad tidings with regard to all the above.

It would also be appropriate for you to give several cents to *tzedakah* prior to your morning and afternoon prayers (except for *Shabbos* and *Yom Tov* as is self-understood).

I hope and am sure that you will accept my proposal and directives as stated above, and you will inform me about all this as soon as possible.

With blessings for good health and a speedy recovery so that you are able to fulfill your mission in this world for many long and good years in peace of mind and tranquility of body, and that you be a chassid.

(Igros Kodesh, Vol. V, p. 176)

LEAVE THE HEALING AND THOUGHTS
ABOUT THE METHODS OF HEALING TO THE DOCTORS

... I have already responded to a number of individuals who had queries like yours [and worried far too much about their health status,] that although on the one hand one is obligated to follow the instructions of the doctor, as explained in many places and also cited as a point of law among the laws of *Shabbos* and

---

14. *Tehillim* 100:2.

circumcision, on the other hand, this only applies to actual performance [of the doctor's orders].

This does not apply, however, to one's focusing his mind on [the intricacies of] his physical ailment, [which should not be done,] since this is not within the individual's area of expertise. ...

[Thinking such thoughts] therefore falls under the heading of useless thoughts that bring no benefit and only serve to confuse the person, for this keeps the mind from thinking about what it should be thinking about, and keeps it thinking about those things which it should not be thinking about.

This [same answer that I gave to others] applies to you as well: Regarding your actual conduct, you are to fulfill the instructions of the doctors, while you are to place your trust in G-d that "He will send forth His [healing] word and heal you."[15] ...

(Igros Kodesh, Vol. IX, p. 272)

LEAVE THE DELVING AND SCRUTINIZING
TO THE DOCTOR

... You write about the [unfortunate] state of your health and that this has caused you to become despondent:

You are surely aware that such conduct is contrary to our Torah in general and *Toras HaChassidus* in particular. While the Torah has granted permission to the healer to heal, the person must simultaneously remember and know full well that G-d is the [ultimate] "Healer of all flesh and Performer of wonders."

Thus, you should serve Him with joy and gladness of heart, and [on His part,] He will surely fulfill His promise of fulfilling the needs of those who serve Him, as explained in many places in *Chassidus*.

---

15 *Tehillim* 107:20: "He sent forth His word and healed them...."

You should not delve at all in [thoughts about] the state of your health, scrutinizing how you feel — this belongs to the doctor and not to the patient. And I surely need not go on at length about something so simple and obvious. ...

(*Igros Kodesh*, Vol. X, p. 198)

Visit the Doctor — Cease Your Conjectures

... With regard to your health:

I have already told many of *Anash* that in situations such as these, regarding what to *do* — one should obey the instructions of the doctor. It follows that one should be checked by a doctor who will then instruct him in a course of action. However, one's concentration and even one's superficial thoughts should not be about one's health situation at all.

Particularly with regard to you, there is absolutely nothing to worry or fret about. However, it would seem from your letter that you are doing the exact opposite: you delve deeply and immerse yourself into thoughts [such as] "How am I feeling today? How was I feeling yesterday? How will I be feeling tomorrow and the day after?" And you end up with outrageous conjectures.

On the other hand, you refuse to visit a doctor, and thus it is impossible for you to do what he tells you.

Since you have already conducted yourself in the above manner for many months [to no avail,] maybe you will now begin to conduct yourself in the manner I suggested above — and in both aspects, [i.e., visiting a doctor and obeying his instructions, and ceasing your conjectures and worries].

(*Likkutei Sichos*, Vol. XXXVI, p. 287[16])

---

16. From a letter of the Rebbe, dated 18 Tammuz, 5715.

THE PATIENT'S ROLE AND RESPONSIBILITY IN HEALING

I have already told you numerous times that among the best advice to speed your healing is [the following]:

a) Be unmindful [to your situation, i.e., do not brood and mope about it]; b) [live in a constant state of] joy.

Both these matters are entirely in your hands and not in the doctor's.

(From a handwritten response of the Rebbe)

CONCENTRATE YOUR THOUGHTS ON TORAH STUDY
— LEAVE THE STUDY OF MEDICINE TO THE DOCTORS

I duly received the two letters in which you write about the state of your health. It seems from them that your frame of mind is not as it should be.

You should rest assured and be confident that G-d, "Healer of all flesh and Performer of wonders," will "send His healing words and heal you."

In addition to the above [aspect of having confidence in G-d's healing power,] it is incumbent to make vessels within the framework of nature, meaning, to follow the orders of the doctors. Nevertheless one must make a distinction between the two.

When it comes to following the doctor's orders, you should only employ your power of action, while your power of thought and cogitation [should not be employed in this area] since you are not a doctor.

Since you are not a doctor and your lot is associated with Torah study, you should therefore employ your thoughts exclusively with regard to matters of Torah and *mitzvos*; the debates and deliberations in medical matters are not your affair and it's a shame to squander time on something that is not in your domain.

Since your intellect is of no use regarding the science of medicine, you were surely given the ability to utilize it in another area (which to my thinking is Torah study, etc.). Thus, by focusing on your medical condition, you are denying yourself concentration and reflection in Torah.

This results in a twofold fault — a lack in one area, [i.e., in your concentrating on Torah,] and superfluous thinking in another area, [i.e., in medicine, since this area is not your concern and domain].

When you give this matter but a bit of thought, you will rejoice at G-d's having granted you the opportunity to delve into Torah study — and you should increase your diligence therein. ...

(*Igros Kodesh*, Vol. VI, p. 98)

KNOWING THAT G-D HEALS AND PERFORMS MIRACLES SHOULD BANISH DEJECTION OVER STATE OF ONE'S HEALTH

I was informed by your wife *tichye* about your overall state of health and that you are in the hospital.

It saddened me to hear that you are feeling dejected. It is a wonder that an individual like you should feel that way; surely I need not explain to an eminent individual such as yourself the importance of *bitachon*, particularly since you are among those individuals who personally witnessed open and revealed miracles in their lives, and who is also aware that G-d is "Healer of all flesh and Performer of wonders."

[For you to be so dejected is more than just a wonder,] it is thus a "wonder upon a wonder."

If you were to heed my words, you would cease thinking about medical matters and rest assured and be confident that G-d will send you a speedy recovery. Furthermore, implant within your psyche that there is absolutely no reason for you to be dejected, G-d forbid.

... I hope you will find my above words acceptable, and see to engrave in your heart the comment of the Baal Shem Tov[17] on the verse: "Serve G-d with joy."

With blessings for good health, and waiting to hear glad tidings from you.

(Igros Kodesh, Vol. VI, p. 106)

HESACH HADAAS — ONE OF THE BEST CURATIVES

In reply to your letter of *erev Shabbos Kodesh*, as well as the news conveyed over the phone:

I stand by my position that one of the best curatives regarding health in general and your health in particular is to distract your attention (*hesach hadaas*), [i.e., stop being preoccupied with your health situation].

Since a person's thoughts are always active, distracting one's attention is best achieved by concentrating one's thoughts elsewhere. In light of the command "Serve G-d with joy,"[18] and service of G-d must be constant (as the verse states: "I place G-d before me constantly,"[19] this being the beginning of the four sections both of the *Tur* as well as the *Shulchan Aruch*), it follows that you should meditate on something that leads to joy.

This is so in the simplest sense as well: The first thoughts of a person every day [are thoughts that lead to joy] — in the words of the Alter Rebbe in his *Siddur*, "Immediately upon awakening, [t]he [person] recites, "I give thanks [to You] ... [Your faithfulness is great"] — and can an individual experience any greater joy than recognizing that he is in the presence of the King of kings, "Whose faithfulness is great," etc.?

---

17. That Divine service encompasses all areas of a person's life.
18. *Tehillim* 100:2.
19. *Ibid.* 16:8.

G-d will surely strengthen your health for many long and good years, and as my father-in-law, the Rebbe, would often say: "Good in every possible way" ("*im kol ha'perushim*") — that you be able to continue your regular studies in *Nigleh* and *Chassidus*, and continue disseminating in your surroundings the guidance and customs of the "Luminary of Torah," the Torah of *Chassidus*.

With blessings for good health and contentment (*harchavas hadaas*).

(*Igros Kodesh*, Vol. X, p. 376)

INTERPRET POSITIVELY, NOT PESSIMISTICALLY

With regard to your son's health:

... I am perplexed by the conduct of *Anash*, our chassidic brotherhood *sheyichyu*, who pessimistically interpret ("*machmirim*") the events that transpire in their lives, although they are aware of the aphorism — stated by my father-in-law, the Rebbe, in the name of many of the leaders of *Chabad* — "Think positively, and you will see positive results" ("*Tracht gut, vet zain gut*"). See also *Horayos* (12a): "It is not appropriate [to portend events by establishing signs and omens, since if the omen does not bode well he may become frightened, and this will negatively affect his fortune]."

(*Igros Kodesh*, Vol. III, p. 364)

DO NOT INFLATE SERIOUSNESS OF ILLNESS — "TRACHT GUT"

... I vigorously frown upon the conduct of *Anash*, our chassidic brotherhood, who view with pessimism and inflate [the severity] — both verbally and in writing — of all their aches and illnesses, Heaven forbid.

This is contrary to the desire of our *Nesiim*, for I have heard many times — and in public as well — from my father-in-law, the

Rebbe, in the name of many of the leaders of *Chabad*: "Think positively, and you will see positive results."

Now, if this is true with regard to [mere thoughts], how much more so does this, [i.e., positivism vs. negativism,] apply to speech and to writing/deed, [as speech and deed are so much more concrete than thought].

(Igros Kodesh, Vol. IV, p. 198)

DO NOT BE AN INGRATE

In reply to your letter from the month of Kislev, the Month of Redemption, in which you describe your present [(according to you) lamentable] situation, and also that throughout all the days of your life you have not experienced goodness. You ask that I mention you, your wife, and your children *sheyichyu* for a blessing.

It would seem that you fail to sense the contradiction in your own letter: An individual for whom G-d prepared a wife and then blessed them with children *shlita* and who then says that he has never experienced goodness in his life is being tremendously ungrateful.

Surely this [ingratitude] will not affect the blessings that G-d has shown you until now — but the fact that G-d will continue His blessings and beneficence, and even increase them in the future, should not be a reason for you to continue to be ungrateful.

Hundreds and thousands of people pray every day that they be blessed with children, willing to give away everything for a single son or daughter, and they have yet to have their prayers answered — may G-d bless them with the fulfillment of their heart's desires for good very shortly.

You who have received this blessing — and it would seem [that you were granted this blessing] without too much prayer on your part — do not recognize your treasure and good fortune, and you twice state in your above-mentioned letter [that you have never experienced goodness, etc.]!

Moreover, you conclude that you do not believe — G-d forbid — that you will ever be helped from Above, for it has been decreed — G-d forbid — that all your days will be tragic and wretched!

Surely you understand that I do not mean to imply that your income must remain meager and your health fragile, etc.

I merely want to bring to your attention the possibility that your frail health and skimpy income may result from your total lack of recognition of [the fact that] G-d has blessed you with something much more important than good health and making a very good living — the blessing of sons and daughters who follow in G-d's path.

When, however, one refuses to recognize his clear and revealed blessings from Above, especially when this lack of recognition is so acute that you use such extreme expressions in your letter — then is it a surprise if blessings are not drawn down from Above with regard to your other affairs?

It is my hope that these few lines will suffice to enlighten you so that you view your state of affairs in their true perspective.

When you will begin serving G-d with true and inner joy, then G-d's blessings will surely increase with regard to health and sustenance, as is understood from many places [in the writings of our Sages,] among them in *Zohar* II, p. 184b.

You have no doubt established times for Torah study, both *Nigleh* and *Chassidus,* [or] at least will begin doing so from now on. It would also be appropriate for you to check your *tefillin* as well as the *mezuzos* in your home. Also, give a few cents to *tzedakah* every weekday morning prior to the morning prayers.

(*Igros Kodesh*, Vol. XII, p. 270)

ANGUISH IS ANTITHETICAL TO HUMAN LIFE AND ENDEAVOR

... It pained me to hear that your wife's health is not all that it should be. It is my hope that the medical treatment has been successful and that your peace of mind has returned — for I was also informed that you were distraught and stressed.

Anguish and being overly stressed is antithetical to all areas of human life and endeavor. In the words of our Sages: [20] "One is not to commence his prayers in a state of sorrow ... [but only when one is in a joyful state (from the performance) of a *mitzvah*." This statement] also applies to Torah study, as it is stated [with regard to serving G-d with joy]:[21] "So, too, with regard to Torah law."

Now, the entire life of a Jew on earth is that of prayer and [adherence to, or study of, the] Torah [and thus all aspects of a person's life are to be joyful] — prayer representing the aspect of bringing about the ascent of the lower realms to the higher realms, up to and including uniting, cleaving and unifying with the Creator; and Torah — the aspect of drawing down goodness and holiness from the higher realms to the lower realms. ...

(Igros Kodesh, Vol. XVIII, p. 89)

INTELLECT MUST DOMINATE THE EMOTIONS

In reply to your express letter that I received today as well as to your previous letter, I find it astounding:

a) that you write in a much abbreviated manner about the health situation of ..., when you would originally send me telegrams on a daily basis.

It is well known that taking the "middle road" is the proper approach, as opposed to one that goes to either extreme, [such as sending daily telegrams and then writing all too briefly,] (except

---

20. *Berachos* 31a.
21. *Shabbos* 30b.

for unusual circumstances [when one should go to an extreme], as explained in *Rambam, Hilchos Deos*).

b) that you express yourself in your letters in alarming and panic-stricken terms. Where is the quality of "intellect dominating the emotions"? At the very least one must negate the "emotions reigning over intellect" — a state wherein the emotions cause a self-induced panic.

[Acting in the above manner causes one] to observe events in opposition to the Baal Shem Tov's insistence [that matters be viewed] with joy.

I have previously written to an individual of *Anash*, our chassidic brotherhood, that by combining two rulings of our Torah, the Torah of Life — that a) one must serve G-d with joy; and b) Divine service is [a constant,] "in *all* your ways" — we arrive at the inescapable conclusion that in all circumstances and at all times one is to be joyful.

(This may well be connected with the teaching of the Baal Shem Tov regarding individual Divine providence [extending over all matters] and the explanations offered in *Chassidus* that each and every incident fulfills G-d's will and intent.)

Consequently, we are able to serve G-d even in the way in which we view the health of another, [and] even with regard to the manner of writing about it. And in accordance with that which is written in *Chassidus*, [attaining this state] "is neither too difficult nor too removed from you."[22] On the contrary, "This thing is very near to you."[23]

May G-d will it that from now on you be able to notify me only of glad tidings — and not just for the reasons mentioned above, but that even your innately glum nature (*hamarah*

---

22. *Devarim* 30:11.
23. *Ibid.*:14.

shechorah sheloi) will acknowledge that one should [always] be joyful.

In accordance with the ruling of our Sages:[24] "He who prays on behalf of his friend [and is himself in need of the same thing, is answered first,"] may G-d grant you and your wife *sheyichyu* improved health — and may you be able to inform me about this as well.

(*Igros Kodesh*, Vol. X, p. 42)

DELAY OF TREATMENT IS FOR THE BEST

In reply to your letter in which you write about [your concern regarding] the delay in the medical treatment until the 27th of Adar II:[25]

You are surely aware of the maxim:[26] "All delays are for the good." ...

(*Igros Kodesh*, Vol. XVIII, p. 267)

---

24. *Bava Kama* 92a.
25. The Rebbe's letter is dated 12 Adar II.
26. See *Igros Kodesh*, Vol. VIII, p. 358.

CHAPTER 7

The Relationship Between
Spiritual and Physical Wellness

"A Healthy Spirit in a Healthy Body"

Physical health is so greatly dependent on spiritual health.

If, in the past, emphasis was placed on *"mens sana in corpore sana,"*[1] in our days it is an accepted principle that even a small spiritual defect can cause grievous physical harm. The healthier the spirit and the greater its influence over the physical body — the greater its ability to correct or overcome physical shortcomings.

This is so true that even in many instances that involve physical healing, prescriptions and drugs are considerably more effective if they are accompanied by the patient's strong will and determination to cooperate [and become well]. ...

(From a letter of the Rebbe, dated the 2nd day of *Rosh Chodesh* Tammuz, 5715)

Principles of Physical and Spiritual Health
And Their Interrelationship Should Be Observed

There are those [medical] issues that have already been well [researched and] established as either beneficial or detrimental to one's health: [Consequently,] even a person who is strongly inclined to perform research and experimentation will surely choose [other areas of research] — areas that have not been previously researched.

---

1. "A healthy spirit in a healthy body."

This generally accepted attitude is quite understandable and logical:

Since experts have amply researched these particular areas and have already determined what is good and what is harmful to physical health — moreover, they have also established the best method to further technological advancements in this area — it would be, at best, a waste of time to repeat these already proven experiments.

Additionally, there is no guarantee that mistakes will not be made in the [repetitive] research and one will thereby arrive at erroneous conclusions, with disastrous effects, as has already transpired.

What has been said above in regard to physical health is also true with regard to spiritual health and well-being, as to how the Divine soul can attain perfection and fulfillment.

This is all the more so since spiritual health is generally related to physical health, particularly as far as a Jew is concerned.

(From a letter of the Rebbe)

THE RELATIONSHIP BETWEEN
THE PHYSICAL AND THE SPIRITUAL

I was pleased to receive your letter of May 15th. I also enjoyed reading there about your interest in *Chassidus*, as well as some of your comments and views regarding the above, particularly in reference to the quality of joy.

[To comment on] that which you write, that the feeling of joy is related to the glandular excretion of hormones, etc., that reach the brain together with the flow of blood, and so on:

Since body and soul are totally connected and united, forming one entity, it follows that every phenomenon in the spiritual realm will also result in a physical phenomenon.

I trust that you will agree with me that such a unity within the microcosm [of man,] serving as it does as an analogy and illustration of the true unity found within the macrocosm [of the universe as a whole], is not at all similar to the philosophy of pantheism — which posits that everything is natural and physical — but [that the true definition of unity] is the very opposite: that all is spirituality, and moreover, that all is G-dliness.

In keeping with this, on the verse[2] "one nation on earth," the Alter Rebbe briefly comments: "This means that even in mundane ['earthly'] matters [the Jewish people] will not be separated — G-d forbid — from G-d's true unity [and oneness]" (*Iggeres HaKodesh*, Epistle IX, p. 114a).

It is worth noting that followers of the philosophy of materialism would rejoice — as if they found a great treasure and as if they found proof to their approach — whenever they would find something relating to the psyche [which they felt to be wholly] related to physical phenomena, such as electronic responses, [e.g., brainwaves, etc.].

In truth, not only is there no contradiction between [spiritual and physical phenomena], the contrary is true — that this is the logical result of the absolute truth of G-d's unity, that G-d is One and there is nothing besides Him [which also causes the unity between [spiritual and physical phenomena].

[This means,] not only is there no G-dliness — Heaven forbid — aside from Him, there is also no true existence other than His — this being one of the fundamental concepts of *Toras HaChassidus*, as explained in the Alter Rebbe's *Shaar HaYichud VehaEmunah*. ...

You do not write about what area of medicine you practice, and I would like to know what it is. In any event, it is my hope that when you heal the physical ailments of your patients, you

---

2.   II *Shmuel* 7:23.

also take into account aspects of their spiritual healing —
particularly for those who do not know that they are ailing
spiritually, which makes them in even greater need of healing.

(Igros Kodesh, Vol. XIII, p. 233)

A HEALTHY SOUL — A HEALTHY BODY

In reply to your letter of the 2nd of Sivan in which you
describe your health situation:

I was surprised that you failed to mention anything at all
regarding the health of your soul: sessions of Torah study,
performance of *mitzvos,* and the service of prayer, [all of which are
vital for the soul's good health,] inasmuch as the health of the
body and the health of the soul are interdependent. ...

(Igros Kodesh, Vol. XI, p. 187)

JEWISH SPIRITUAL HEREDITY

... Considering the fact that even secular knowledge now
realizes the importance of heredity to a person's life, you should
therefore explain to the medical students that the health of a
Jew's soul is connected with its inheritance of the Torah received
at Mt. Sinai.

A Jew cannot possibly be mentally and spiritually whole if he
is — Heaven forbid — sundered from the source to which his
parents and grandparents were so closely connected for countless
generations.

(Igros Kodesh, Vol. X, p. 38)

"ALL IS IN THE HANDS OF HEAVEN
EXCEPT FOR THE FEAR OF HEAVEN"

... You write that you do not know what it is that you want
and what you are lacking:

This seems to contradict what you wrote at the beginning of your letter [about members of your family who are not well and in need of healing, etc.].

Since you write there about family members who are ill and in need of healing, etc. — and there is the known saying of our Sages that the 248 organs and 365 veins of the body correspond to the 248 Positive Commandments and the 365 Negative Commandments — it is thus understandable that illness of the body is also remedied by health of the soul.

Thus, adding in vitality in matters of the soul enhances one's physical life as well and increases the success of medical treatment.

Moreover, while when it comes to physical health we beseech G-d to heal us, for "All is in the hands of Heaven,"[3] however, when it comes to the soul's health the Torah has informed us that this is left up to our free choice — "[All is in the hands of Heaven,] except for the fear of Heaven."[4]

From this we understand that nothing can stand in the way of your fierce and powerful desire to ascend spiritually and increase in Torah, going from strength to strength. May G-d will it that you convey good news concerning all the above.

(*Igros Kodesh*, Vol. XVII, p. 242)

IMPROVING ONE'S PHYSICAL AND SPIRITUAL HEALTH

... It is well known that according to our Torah, the Torah of Life, whenever there is something within the body that needs improvement, it is accomplished both through physical as well as spiritual remedies. ...

(From a letter of the Rebbe)

---

3.   *Berachos* 33b, *et al.*

4.   *Ibid.*

ACHIEVING HARMONY BETWEEN BODY AND SOUL

It pleased me to receive your letter of the 15th of Shevat, the "New Year for Trees." There are many well-known passages in books of homiletics (*drush*) regarding the inspiration that can be drawn from this day, based on the phrase in the verse:[5] "For man is a tree of the field."

When someone becomes spiritually healthier he automatically becomes physically healthier as well, for Jews are "the one nation on earth,"[6] which is to say that wherever they are, they implement the concept of oneness, and included in that is the conception of the overall unity of matter and spirit, body and soul.

This, too, is one of the explanations of the philosophical system of the Baal Shem Tov, that of serving G-d joyfully together with the body — not by afflicting the body, but by using the body as an active partner in one's Divine service.

We readily observe that when the body is healthy — understandably, in a Jewish manner, by eating kosher foods, etc. — the body does not hinder the study of Torah and performance of *mitzvos*, should the person truly desire to do so.

According to the well-known saying of our Sages, [7]of blessed memory, regarding achieving peace between body and soul, and within the soul as well: peace between the Divine soul and the animal soul,[8] this peace also leads to peace in one's own immediate and close surroundings, as well as to peace in distant places, and ultimately to world peace.

All the above leads to the true state of peace [that will take place with *Mashiach's* arrival,] concerning which time the prophet

---

5.   *Devarim* 20:19.
6.   II *Shmuel* 7:23.
7.   See *Sanhedrin* 99b.
8.   *Ibid.*

Yeshayahu states:[9] "Nation will not lift sword against nation, and they will study warfare no more." ...

(*Igros Kodesh*, Vol. XXI, p. 335)

MAKING VESSELS FOR G-D'S BLESSINGS

... It pleased me to hear today the good news that your operation was successful. May G-d help that your condition consistently improves so that you are able to convey the tidings that you are fully recovered.

However, in order to receive G-d's blessings one must prepare the proper vessels to contain these Divine blessings. For a Jew these vessels are Torah and *mitzvos*; I hope you will undertake to increase — *bli neder* — their performance.

The more intense and frequent your actions, the greater will be the blessings G-d sends you and the speedier will you receive them.

I want to suggest that you scrupulously observe putting on *tefillin* daily, and following the prayers recite a few chapters of *Tehillim*. Prior to putting on *tefillin*, give a few francs to *tzedakah*.

(*Igros Kodesh*, Vol. V, p. 183)

INCREASING TORAH STUDY, PERFORMANCE OF MITZVOS AND SERVICE OF PRAYER

You write to me about the state of your health:

There is the known directive of our Torah, the Torah of Life, on the verse "and he shall heal,"[10] that "Permission was granted the healer to heal."[11] You should therefore fulfill the instructions of a physician who specializes in healing your ailment.

---

9.   *Yeshayahu* 2:4.
10. *Shemos* 21:19.
11. *Berachos* 60a.

However, at the same time, you must clearly know that G-d is the "Healer of all flesh and Performer of wonders";[12] the individual physician and specific medication are merely His agents and instruments.

Therefore, first and foremost you should improve and strengthen your spiritual health. In turn, this will enhance[13] "your cleaving to G-d," through which "you are all alive today," with manifest life and good health, extending to all your bodily limbs.

Increase your diligence and assiduousness in your study of Torah and performance of *mitzvos* in a most beautiful and meticulous manner (*b'hiddur*), as well as your service of prayer.

Understandably, all the above can be done without taking away from your health; there is enough time in the day to occupy yourself both in increasing the health of your soul and the health of your body. When you do so, [i.e., increase your Torah study, performance of *mitzvos*, and service of prayer,] you will feel physically better as well.

(Igros Kodesh, Vol. X, p. 36)

"Be Whole With the L-rd, Your G-d"

... We readily observe that improving one's spiritual health literally improves one's physical health as well.

Thus the verse commands: "Be whole with the L-rd, your G-d"[14] — "whole" in one's spiritual and physical 248 bodily organs and 365 veins, corresponding as they do to the 248 Positive Commandments and the 365 Negative Commandments,[15] and as the Alter Rebbe explains this verse.[16]

(Igros Kodesh, Vol. XV, p. 150)

---

12. From the text of the "*Asher Yatzar*" blessing, from *Berachos* 60b.
13. *Devarim* 4:4.
14. *Devarim* 18:13.
15. *Zohar I*, p. 170b.
16. In *Likkutei Torah, Nitzavim*, p. 45c.

FEELING "BETTER AND HEALTHIER"
IS A COMBINATION OF BODY AND SPIRIT

I was sorry to hear that you have not been feeling up to par recently.

I trust that this letter will find you in improved health; may G-d grant you a speedy and complete recovery so that you will be able to continue your good work for a better and happier environment, in good health and with joy and gladness of heart.

If you suspect that by saying a "better and happier environment" I have not only your professional and scientific work in mind, but also something that has to do with Torah and *mitzvos*, you are quite right — for Torah is the true good, the source of true happiness.

(From a letter of the Rebbe, in the year 5724)

INTERDEPENDENCY OF THE
SPIRITUAL AND PHYSICAL ASPECTS OF THE JEW

Surely you will not withhold glad tidings from me and you will inform me about the health of ..., as well as the spiritual health of everybody [in the community].

This is in keeping with the saying of our Sages, of blessed memory, that the 248 Positive Commandments correspond to man's 248 bodily organs and the 365 Negative Commandments correspond to the person's 365 veins.

You understand no doubt that this is not a mere similarity of numbers, but that a person's organs receive their life-force through performing positive commands. So, too, a person's veins are clear and healthy and the blood flows through them properly by not transgressing the 365 prohibitory commands.

For it is readily understood that the spiritual and physical aspects of the Jew are not two distinct and separate entities, but are truly one; [and] one is dependent on the other.

All the above is hinted at in a concise manner in *Likkutei Torah*[17] of the Alter Rebbe, author of the *Tanya* and *Shulchan Aruch*.

(*Igros Kodesh*, Vol. VII, p. 19)

PREPARING VESSELS FOR G-D'S BLESSINGS

... As you may know, in order to receive G-d's blessings, it is necessary to prepare proper "vessels." While it would have been impossible for us to know on our own which are the proper vessels for His blessings, G-d in His infinite mercy and kindness revealed to us in His Torah that Torah and *mitzvos* are the proper vessels for us to receive His blessings.

Not knowing you personally, it is difficult for me to indicate how you can make such additional vessels for yourself in order to receive G-d's blessings; the important thing, however, is to enhance your religious observance. This will surely result in an improvement in your condition.

(From a letter of the Rebbe, dated the 4th of Shvat, 5713)

CREATING VESSELS FOR DIVINE BLESSINGS
SHOULD BE DONE UNCONDITIONALLY

I received your letter in which you notify me about Mr. ... and his wife *sheyichyu*. [You write to me that] he is suffering from a number of ailments and his wife is also not well. You ask for a blessing on their behalf:

Explain to them that G-d, the King of kings, is the sole Master of the entire universe, and that He is the Essence of goodness, kindness and mercy. We on our part have merely to make the proper vessels in order to draw down and receive His blessings from on High. The appropriate vessels for a Jewish man and woman are matters of Torah and *mitzvos*.

---

17. *Devarim*, p. 45c.

When someone is physically hungry or thirsty, he stills his hunger with bread and quenches his thirst with water; it does not matter whether or not he understands how the bread and water are able to satisfy his hunger and slake his thirst.

The same is true regarding one's spiritual life. When the soul hungers and thirsts for the bread and water of Torah and *mitzvos*, the most important thing is the actual deed — that its hunger and thirst be slaked through the practical performance of Torah and *mitzvos*.

Once the soul becomes healthier and stronger, it will be much simpler — and a lot less time-consuming as well — for it to understand [the significance of] Torah and *mitzvos*. Moreover, this will [not only be apprehended by his soul, but] even by his [inherently] limited physical intellect.

However, one should not change the order and declare that only after he understands the why's and wherefore's [of the necessity of observing Torah and *mitzvos*] will he be ready to observe them.

All the above also applies to Mr. ... *sheychye*. G-d will surely return him to good health. But he on his part should not make conditions that first he must get well and only then will he use his free time to understand the necessity of performing Torah and *mitzvos*, and only [then] begin increasing his practical performance of Torah and *mitzvos*.

To act in the above manner is similar to someone who is unwell and yet insists that he will not take any medication until he concludes studying the science of medicine and understands exactly how the medication promotes his healing.

In point of fact, it is quite the contrary: Taking medicine will strengthen his intellect, making it much easier for him to understand the science of medicine [and how the medication promotes his healing].

Mr. ... should begin performing *mitzvos*, particularly wearing *tefillin* and observing *kashrus*, and his wife should begin conducting a scrupulously kosher home and lighting candles prior to *Shabbos* and Festivals, and before lighting them she should give to the charity of R. Meir Baal HaNes.

[When they will begin doing so,] they will merit to be able in a short amount of time to convey glad tidings about an improvement in their health.

(Igros Kodesh, Vol. V, p. 314)

SEEK SPIRITUAL REMEDIES AS WELL AS PHYSICAL REMEDIES

In reply to your letter in which you write about [the poor health of] your daughter *tichye*:

With regard to a Jew — as a member of our nation termed "a unique nation on earth,"[18] which as the Alter Rebbe notes (*Iggeres HaKodesh*, Epistle 9), means that "even 'earthly' matters do not separate them from G-d's unity" — concurrent with actions done via natural means [to bring about healing,] one must engage in spiritual actions as well. Generally speaking, this means that one is to increase his performance of Torah and *mitzvos*.

My intent in "engage in spiritual actions as well" is that first and foremost you should ascertain whether your daughter was born in purity, i.e., whether you and your wife observed then the laws of family purity and immersion in a *mikveh*.

I trust you will not be offended by this comment of mine, for since I do not know you personally, and with regard to the health of a Jewish person there is no room for misplaced embarrassment, I have therefore mentioned the matter cited above.

If, G-d forbid, something was lacking in your observance of this matter, then in addition to being scrupulous in your observance of the laws of family purity in the future, you are to

---

18. *II Shmuel* 7:23.

encourage others as well to increase their observance of family purity. This will rectify, at least to some extent, the above matter.

Whatever the case may be, it would be appropriate for your wife *tichye* to set aside some coins before lighting candles every *erev Shabbos* and *erev Yom Tov*, and you should also do the same prior to your morning prayers on Mondays and Thursdays.

Following the morning prayers, recite the daily portion of *Tehillim* as divided by the days of the month; also check the *mezuzos* in your home to ascertain their *kashrus*.

May G-d grant that you be able to convey glad tidings with regard to all the above, particularly about the improvement in your daughter's *tichye*'s health. ...

(Igros Kodesh, Vol. IX, p. 91)

TWO FORMS OF SPIRITUAL AND PHYSICAL HEALING

... It is known that in general, healing only cures an illness from the moment of the cure and on (*Kesuvos* 74b), [but we cannot say that the person was not previously ill]. However it is possible for healing to be so potent that it is as if the illness never occurred in the first place (see *Chulin* 48a, Responsa of the *Tzafnas Panei'ach* 1:14).

The life and health of the body are dependent on the soul, and the life and health of the Jew's soul depends on his performance of Torah and *mitzvos*, as per the saying of our Sages, of blessed memory: the 248 bodily organs correspond to the 248 Positive Commandments, and the 365 veins correspond to the 365 Negative Commandments (*Zohar* I, p. 170b).

This [above correlation between the number of commandments and the organs and veins of the body] is not merely a quantitative similarity; on the contrary — because of their inner relationship their number is the same as well (see *Tanya*, ch. 51).

When it comes to the person's spiritual healing, the "healing of the soul" — from which emanates man's physical healing — these two manners of healing are to be found as well: [One is] whether the person rectifies [through his repentance] his situation, [i.e., his spiritual malady,] from that point on only, [and the other is] whether he uproots [his spiritual malady] from the very beginning, [i.e., that it did not exist at all].

The difference between these two forms [of repentance and spiritual healing] depends on whether the person's service [and repentance] is out of fear [of G-d,] or out of love [for Him] (*Yoma* 86a).

When one serves out of love, then no vestige of his former improper spiritual state remains and the person returns to his full spiritual and physical strength and vigor, for the aspect of the "strength of the soul," [i.e., his soul's essence,] also assists the body in returning to its full and undiminished strength (see *Kuntres Acharon* in *Tanya*, titled *U'Tzedakah K'Nachal Eisan*, and *Likkutei Torah*, the discourse titled, "I am placing a blessing before you today," the beginning of the section *Re'eh*).

(*Igros Kodesh*, Vol. VII, p. 47)

LESSON OF TEFILLIN
FOR SPIRITUAL AND PHYSICAL HEALTH

... Rabbi ... informed me that you are a doctor. Surely then I need not impress upon you that a person's physical health is connected with his spiritual health. You also, therefore, don't need elaborate explanations about how important it is for a Jew's soul to receive what it requires, i.e., matters of Torah and *mitzvos*. Only then can the physical body be healthy as well.

This is also one of the explanations and meanings of the *mitzvah* of putting on *tefillin*, which are placed on the head wherein is found the brain, and upon [that part of] the hand [which is] opposite the heart. All the nerves of the body are connected to the brain and the entire body receives its blood from the heart.

The *tefillin* contain four sections of the Torah, beginning with the verse: "Hear O Israel, G-d is our L-rd, G-d is One." This is the call to every Jew that he hear and remember that G-d is the sole Master of all, including the person's private life.

When this knowledge permeates and pervades one's mind and heart, then the person's entire body and soul are healthy. ...

(*Igros Kodesh*, Vol. IX, p. 105)

KEEP YOUR PROMISES AND FULFILL YOUR PLEDGES

... It would be beneficial to motivate your son-in-law to fulfill the pledge that he willingly made regarding improving his performance of Torah and *mitzvos* if her[19] health improves. Why should he wait for warnings from Above [to do so?] ...

(*Igros Kodesh*, Vol. XXI, p. 135)

SPECIAL EFFORTS BY WOMEN
TO RECEIVE G-D'S BLESSINGS FOR HEALTH
AS THEY CAN ACCOMPLISH MORE THAN MEN

... You should, however, explain to her that in order to receive and retain G-d's blessings, she must make the proper vessels for them — vessels that G-d has said bring life, health and sustenance for Jews, both for men and women, old and young.

These [vessels] are the commandments that G-d gave us on Mount Sinai, commandments that are to be performed at all times and in all places — particularly by women, who in many areas can accomplish more than men.

---

19. Most probably referring to the wife's health.

It is therefore very important for her to possess those vessels — *mitzvos* — that she is still lacking, and enhance and beautify those vessels — *mitzvos* — that she already has.

That is to say she should now begin observing those *mitzvos* that she did not observe until now, and that those *mitzvos* that she does observe should be observed with greater vitality and pleasure from now on.

This will hasten G-d blessings for herself and her family.

(Igros Kodesh, Vol. VI, p. 304)

"HEART TO HEART"

In response to your letter of Tuesday, where you write to me about your general state of health and about your heart condition:

There is the well-known saying of our Sages, of blessed memory, that the 248 Positive Commandments correspond to a person's 248 bodily organs, and the 365 Negative Commandments correspond to the person's 365 veins.

The import of this statement is that a Jew's physical body, its various aspects and its general health, are dependent on the condition of his spiritual body — his level and standing in performing Positive Commandments and refraining from transgressing Negative Commandments.

G-d desired that the world we are in be created in a lowly state, clothed in physicality, and whose external conduct — as seen by the human eye — is of a natural order. Consequently, many matters in this world [such as healing and good health] require [not only a spiritual approach, but] a physical approach as well.

It is understood from the above that we should obey the instructions of our doctors, in accordance with the saying of our Sages: "Permission was granted the healer to heal."

At the same time, however, we must always be aware that it is G-d Who creates, sustains and enlivens the world and all of its creatures, especially the children of Avraham, Yitzchak and Yaakov, concerning whom the verse states: "You are children to the L-rd, your G-d."[20]

Since G-d is the "Essence of goodness"[21] and "it is the nature of one who is good to act benevolently," there is no reason — Heaven forbid — for worry, and thus a person can carry out his work and service with great joy and with true joy, [i.e., not only immense joy but joy based on principles of truth, that there is truly something to be joyous about].

All the above applies to you as well. Be assured that your heart is receptive and responsive to G-d and His Torah and *mitzvos* — thus you will merit many long and pleasant days and years.

Nevertheless, in order to merit an increased measure of Divine blessings and success, you should increase your generosity to others — increasing your actual charitable giving, as well as acting benevolently toward others, physically as well as spiritually, by drawing them closer to Torah and *mitzvos*. And [you should know that] "There is nothing that stands in the way of one's desire."[22]

(Igros Kodesh, Vol. XII, p. 353)

---

20. *Devarim* 14:1.
21. *Likkutei Sichos*, Vol. XXIV, p. 334.
22. *Zohar* II, p. 162b.

CHAPTER 8

Specific Spiritual Assists
To Health and Healing

TORAH STUDY

INCREASE IN TORAH — INCREASE IN LIFE

Surely I need not draw your attention to the deeper meaning of the concept that the Jewish people are "the one nation on earth"[1] — not only the simple meaning that Jews believe in one G-d and in one Torah, but that they draw down unity [("oneness")] into all aspects of this world.

This is to say that there is no disunity and plurality within this world at all: just as G-d is one with an utter and simple unity, so, too, is unity and singularity found within all worldly aspects, particularly since the physical and the spiritual are not separate entities, but are truly one. It's just that G-d allowed for the possibility [for man to believe the opposite of the truth] — as our Sages, of blessed memory, say: "Let he who *desires* to be mistaken come and be mistaken."[2]

This is part of the mission of the Jew: that he himself understand and sense G-d's unity and make this aspect of Divine unity understood to those in his surroundings, and, to the greatest extent possible, to all those upon whom he has influence.

---

1.   *II Shmuel* 7:23.
2.   *Bereishis Rabbah* 8:8.

The same holds true with regard to one's health: When one needs to improve and increase his physical health and well-being, he should do so in conjunction with and with a concurrent and corresponding increase in his spiritual health and well-being — in the words of our Sages: "Whoever will increase, will see an increase."[3]

In light of the above, I am taking the liberty to bring to your awareness that it would be beneficial for your father *shlita* to increase his study sessions in our Torah, the Torah of Life.

It is through Torah that "He has implanted in us eternal life."[4] One of the meanings of this passage is that even though we live within this corporeal world, we live a true [eternal] life — something that should be felt within one's physical body as well.

This is also in keeping with the ruling of the *Rambam* in *Hilchos Deos*, the beginning of ch. 4, where he states that "maintaining a healthy and whole body is an integral part of Divine service."

(Igros Kodesh, Vol. VII, p. 141)

"TORAH BRINGS HEALING"

Surely you will find the right words with which to explain to ... that his response of "I am entirely incapable of learning Torah at present because I am in pain," is similar to one who is ill and refuses to take medication with the excuse that he is ill.

Similarly, our Sages, of blessed memory, have informed us that "Torah brings healing to the world," and "He whose head or body aches should study Torah."[5]

While it is understandable that in-depth study is difficult while one is in pain, an effort should nevertheless be made.

---

3.   *Taanis* 31a.
4.   Blessing after the Torah reading.
5.   *Eruvin* 54a.

Surely, one can at least study with less concentration — at least [study and recite] the three well-known daily lessons that apply to all, those of *Chumash*, *Tehillim* and *Tanya*, as established by my father-in-law, the Rebbe.

May G-d will it that you be able to convey glad tidings to me, and that your words that "come from the heart" enter the heart of ..., and that they accomplish their desired result.

(Igros Kodesh, Vol. XV, p. 175)

TORAH — PARTICULARLY CHITAS — IS THE VESSEL FOR RECEIVING ALL DIVINE BLESSINGS INCLUDING HEALTH

I received your *pidyon nefesh* in which you ask that Divine mercy be aroused for you so that you should be in good health. I will read the *pidyon nefesh* at the holy resting place of my father-in-law, the Rebbe, for the fulfillment of your heart's desire for good in all that you require.

It is known that in order to receive blessings from on High, we must create here below, [i.e., in this physical world,] the proper vessels into which these blessings will flow. Torah is the [most appropriate] vehicle for receiving any and all blessings.

I therefore suggest that you take upon yourself — *bli neder* — the observance of the three daily lessons [known as *Chitas*], established by my father-in-law, the Rebbe, an observance that applies to all *Anash*, our chassidic brotherhood.

They are: the daily portion of *Tehillim* as divided by the days of the month, recited following the morning prayers; the daily section of the weekly Torah portion — on Sunday, from the beginning of the portion to *Sheni*, on Monday from *Sheni* to *Shelishi*, and so on; and *Tanya*, as divided by the days of the year.

Observance of the above will surely serve as a fit vehicle to draw down and receive G-d's blessings.

(Igros Kodesh, Vol. V, p. 51)

TORAH STUDY AS AN AID TO VARIOUS AILMENTS

Our Sages, of blessed memory, [state] in *Eruvin* 54a, that "If one has a headache he should study Torah, and if one has a sore throat he should study Torah." The *Gemara* concludes that when he does so, he will be healed.

The question [regarding this statement] is simple: We observe people who have headaches and study Torah and are not relieved of their headaches.

Of the many answers that are provided to the above question, one of them is that Torah is an entire organism, as it states:[6] "This is the Torah — *man*." [Just as man is an organic whole, so too is Torah.]

Torah thus contains some elements that relate to the head and other elements that relate to the throat, etc. Thus, when one has a headache, he should study Torah. If G-d blesses him with good fortune and he happens upon that section of Torah that relates to the head, then he will be healed of his headache.

Not everyone, however, is spiritually clear-sighted enough to find the appropriate section of Torah that provides healing for one's headache, or the specific portion of Torah that relieves one's sore throat, etc. ...

(Igros Kodesh, Vol. V, p. 53)

TORAH AND CONTINUED GOOD HEALTH

... We find ourselves now in the days preceding [Shavuos, the festival of] receiving the Torah, which brings healing to the world as a whole and the Jewish people — the receivers of the Torah — in particular.

In light of that which is known — that in a more particular sense we receive the Torah anew every day, as emphasized by the

---

6. *Bamidbar* 19:14.

fact that the phrase "Giver of the Torah" is in present tense — we understand that a Jew must be healthy and whole each and every day. In the words of the *Rambam*: "Maintaining a healthy and whole body is an integral part of Divine service."

... Surely I need not motivate you to influence your son to establish set times for the study of the inner portion of Torah (*pnimiyus haTorah*), which in our generation has been revealed in *Toras HaChassidus*.

Every increase in Torah and *mitzvos*, and surely adding to the study of *pnimiyus haTorah*, which is termed in the *Zohar* the "soul of Torah," greatly increases G-d's blessings for all of one's personal needs, both for the life of the body as well as for the life of the soul.

(Igros Kodesh, Vol. XVII, p. 129)

DELAYING TORAH STUDY PENDING GOOD HEALTH
IS SIMILAR TO
DELAYING TAKING MEDICATION UNTIL ONE IS WELL

In reply to your letter of the 12th of Menachem Av, I hope and pray to G-d that your health will soon improve.

Regarding your statement that it is difficult for you to maintain your established times for Torah study [due to your illness]: This is just like an ill person saying that he cannot take his prescribed medications for he is not yet well [and he will only begin taking them after he is healed].

...Established times for studying the Torah of my father-in-law, the Rebbe, הכ״מ, are a vehicle through which one draws down his blessings for good health and sustenance.

Thus, if one laments his [meager] sustenance and [poor] health, the means [for improving them] is strengthening the established times for study. Thereby, [his] sustenance and health will be as they should be. ...

(Igros Kodesh, Vol. III, p. 381)

TZEDAKAH

THE MOST IMPORTANT MEDICINE FOR A JEW —
TZEDAKAH, GOOD DEEDS AND A CHAPTER OF TEHILLIM

... Your son *sheyichye* told me that your daughter ... is not, for the time being, in the best of health. No doubt she went to a doctor and is following his instructions.

In addition to your daughter's conduct of lighting candles prior to *Shabbos* and Festivals, she should — until she reaches the age of eighteen — place three coins in a charity box of R. Meir Baal HaNes prior to candle lighting. It would also be advisable that you recite ch. 71 in *Tehillim* every day until Rosh HaShanah.

Your son *sheyichye* also told me that his aunt ... is not in the best of health. She too should be told what I stated above; i.e., to obey the instructions of the medical specialist and place three coins in a charity box of R. Meir Baal HaNes prior to candle lighting. Additionally, at least once a week, she should provide a Jew with a meal (a guest or a poor person).

Healing is done by G-d; He does this in part through [the medium of] a doctor. However, He established that the *principal* medicine for a Jew is *tzedakah*, good deeds and a chapter of *Tehillim*. ...

(Igros Kodesh, Vol. III, p. 359)

SUPPORTING A TORAH STUDENT —
AN APT VESSEL FOR RECEIVING G-D'S BLESSINGS
FOR GOOD HEALTH

... In order for G-d's blessings to be long lasting, it is necessary to provide the proper vessels (the medium through which one gathers in [these blessings]), these vessels being [the study of] Torah and [the performance of] *mitzvos*.

My opinion therefore is that [since the two of you are in need of a blessing for healing,] you should both take upon yourself to support a young man or young lady who studies in one of the Israeli institutions named after my father-in-law, the Rebbe, of blessed memory.

You, Mrs. ..., should give *tzedakah* for the charity of R. Meir Baal HaNes prior to candle lighting *erev Shabbos*, and you, Mr. ..., should recite several chapters of *Tehillim* each morning following prayers — at least the daily portion of *Tehillim* as divided by the days of the month.

It would also be most appropriate to have the *mezuzos* of your home checked to make sure they are kosher according to Jewish law.

(Igros Kodesh, Vol. V, p. 225)

Donating to the Charity of Bikkur Cholim

Surely you have regular study sessions in both the revealed and mystical portions of Torah and you also recite the daily portion of *Tehillim* (as divided by the days of the month).

It would be most beneficial for you to give several coins to the charity of *Bikkur Cholim* [the charity of visiting and attending to the ill,] each Monday and Thursday prior to your morning prayers.

(Igros Kodesh, Vol. VIII, p. 111)

DO NOT GO BACK ON YOUR WORD[7]

Explain to his wife that in his present situation, *Heaven forbid* he should go back on his promise to give *tzedakah* — [for doing so means renouncing his promise] to G-d, [and it is] *He* who is the Healer of all flesh (while human doctors are but His agents). ...

(*Likkutei Sichos*, Vol. XXXVI, p. 299)

DO NOT MAKE PRECONDITIONS WITH G-D

... I must comment about what you write at the conclusion of your letter, that when, with G-d's help, your daughter will become well then you will — *bli neder* — donate to *Yeshivas Tomchei Temimim*:

It is incorrect to use such terminology and make conditions with G-d that first He must help and [only] then, etc.

A Jew is to do all he can in matters of Torah and *mitzvos* — and the *mitzvah* of *tzedakah* is included therein, and what's more, *tzedakah* is equivalent to all other *mitzvos*, so much so, that when using the generic term "*mitzvah*," reference is being made to *tzedakah* (see *Tanya*, ch. 37 at length).

At the same time, one is to pray, supplicate and demand of G-d that He fulfill his needs in the areas of children, life and ample sustenance.

(*Igros Kodesh*, Vol. XV, p. 400)

TZEDAKAH BY BOTH PARENT AND CHILD

To a parent whose child was having mental problems, the Rebbe advised:

---

7. The above is the Rebbe's reply to an individual who sought the Rebbe's blessing for a wealthy individual suffering from cancer. He received the Rebbe's blessing and the individual was healed. Having been healed, he pledged a large sum to *tzedakah*. Later, however, under pressure from his family, he retracted his pledge.

It would be good to set aside a couple of cents for *tzedakah* every weekday morning, and that you and your daughter personally place the money into the *tzedakah* box. Of course, there should be no compulsion [to do so, i.e., do not force your daughter to personally give the *tzedakah* if she is resistant to this suggestion].

It would also be advisable to have the *mezuzos* checked.

(From a letter of the Rebbe, dated the 12th of Adar, 5718)

KASHRUS

THE BENEFICIAL EFFECTS OF KEEPING KOSHER

I was pleased to be informed about your steady advancement in matters of Torah, called *Toras Chayim*, [the Torah of Life], because it is the Jew's guide in life, and also *Toras Emes*, [the Torah of Truth], because it is the truth.

This is doubly gratifying since people of your standing have an impact on the community, for people look up to you and try to emulate you. Thus, your going from strength to strength in matters of Torah and *mitzvos* is greatly multiplied through those who are inspired by your example, not to mention the direct impact on children and through them on their children in an everlasting chain reaction.

In light of the above, even if there are some difficulties to overcome, it is surely worthwhile to make the effort, since the effort only involves the individual, while the outcome benefits many.

Also, add to this the fact that this is also the channel to receive G-d's blessings in all needs, and that G-d rewards in kind and in a most generous measure.

The above refers to all matters of Torah and *mitzvos*, but has a special significance in regard to *kashrus*.

As a doctor you know the immense knowledge that has been accumulated recently in the area of diet and nutrition, and how much the quality of food affects physical and mental health. For Jews, the dietary laws have come down with the Torah itself, [the Torah having] revealed the true meaning of monotheism of which the Jewish People have been the bearers ever since.

The Torah was relevant not only in those days of old, when paganism and idolatry were the general practice in the world, but it is just as relevant in the present day and age, since it is only the Torah and *mitzvos* that are the basis of pure monotheism, rooted in the absolute unity of G-d.

This means that the Jew brings unity and harmony into the physical world, eliminating any departmentalization in daily life, or practicing one's religion only occasionally; or, as some misguided and misconceived individuals might think, that they can practice Judaism at home but must make concessions and compromises outside the home.

All such differentiations are contrary to true unity, pure monotheism. For the concept of pure monotheism is not just confined to the idea that there is One G-d, but at the same it also requires unity in the personal life of each and every Jew, who is a member of the "one people," of which it is said that they are "one people on earth."

According to the explanation of the Alter Rebbe, founder of *Chabad*, "one people on earth" means that they also bring oneness and unity in earthly things, and it is only in this way that the individual can achieve complete personal harmony and unity of the body and soul, at all times, whether in the synagogue, at home, or in the office.

Thus, the importance of *kashrus* to a Jew is obvious, since the food and beverages that he consumes become blood and tissue and energy, and food that is not suitable (kosher) for a Jew can only alienate him from matters of *Yiddishkeit*, [Judaism]. Only proper and kosher food can nourish the Jew physically, mentally and spiritually.

As already mentioned, there is no need to elaborate on this to you, a physician, even though your specialty is not directly in the field of nutrition.

The most desirable blessing that can be expressed in this case is that you should indeed serve as a living and inspiring example for others to emulate, and that through your inspiration, many others will go from strength to strength in matters of Torah and *mitzvos* in daily life.

(From a letter of the Rebbe)

Proper Observance of Kashrus Benefits Health

I am in receipt of your letter of the 17th of Tammuz, with the enclosure.

If you will let me know the Jewish names, together with the mother's Jewish name — as is customary — of all those [patients] for whom you request a blessing, I will remember them all in prayer.

It is surely unnecessary to emphasize to you at length that since all blessings come from G-d, and the channel to receive them is through daily life and conduct in accordance with His will — namely in accordance with Torah and *mitzvos* — every additional effort in matters of *Yiddishkeit* is bound to widen the channels to receive G-d's blessing.

... With reference to the matter of *kashrus*, which you mention particularly in connection with the assertion that kosher meat available in your area does not taste very good, I trust you will be able to find the proper words to explain (particularly since you are a physician) that proper nutrition has a direct effect not only on physical health, but also on such matters as mood, nerves, thinking, etc., although the latter effects are often more subtle and hidden.

This is patently obvious since nourishment is absorbed within the body and is directly linked to its physical and mental capacities, as has also been confirmed by medical science. [As opposed to nourishment,] taste is merely linked to the palate and is of *very* short duration. The consumption of wholesome and nutritional food is, of course, of lasting vital importance.

As far as a Jew is concerned, our Torah, the Torah of Life, granted to us by the Creator and Master of the Universe, is quite specific as to what a Jew may or may not eat. Only that which is permissible [for a Jew to eat or drink] is truly wholesome and nourishing [for him].

As is the case with all G-d's commandments, they have not been given to us for G-d's benefit, but for our own benefit, and not only for our benefit in the Afterlife, but also in the here and now.

In view of the above, indulgence in taste is surely of little consequence in comparison to the vital importance of observing the Jewish dietary laws in everyday life.

(From a letter of the Rebbe, dated the 24th of Tammuz, 5739)

A THERAPEUTIC KOSHER DIET

... It pleased me to learn that Miss ... refuses to taint herself with non-kosher foods. This itself will enhance her physical health and healing.

On your part, you will surely make an effort to insure that her nourishment be of the best possible quality, as the doctors demand, and at the same time that the foods be kosher.

May G-d send her His "healing words," and heal her speedily.

(*Likkutei Sichos*, Vol. XXXVI, p. 298[8])

---

8.   From a letter of the Rebbe, dated 29 Nissan, 5715.

PHYSICAL, MENTAL AND SPIRITUAL GOOD HEALTH
THROUGH OBSERVANCE OF KASHRUS

It has always been known, and it has been particularly emphasized lately, that diet is very important to the general state of one's physical health and emotional stability. Many books and articles have already been written and continue to be written on this subject by nutritional authorities and physicians who have dedicated their lives to this specialty.

It is now a universally accepted belief that a human being cannot simply eat and drink whatever he desires or whatever tempts him, but must learn to regulate his nutritional intake. Indeed, the endeavor of nutritional experts and dieticians is to prescribe the proper diet of foods and beverages for each individual in accordance with his or her lifestyle, environment, etc.

Typically, research periodically uncovers new findings, [and] very often the latest findings invalidate the previous ones, though it is assumed that in due course these latest findings may similarly be invalidated by even newer findings.

Lay people can only follow the advice of the experts — as long as they are trustworthy — and willingly accept the restrictions they impose [on the individual for reasons of health. So important is their counsel, that people] even pay for their advice, and so on.

Needless to say, all this is as it should be, since not everyone has the time or capacity to do the research to determine what is good for him physically and spiritually.

In light of the above, how grateful must a Jew be to G-d, the Creator of the world and the Essence of Perfection, Who is certainly trustworthy, for His directives in this field, by giving us our dietary laws, the laws of *kashrus*, which ensure our good health physically, mentally and spiritually.

(From a letter of the Rebbe, in the year 5736)

... Thus it is obvious how important *kashrus* is for a Jew, since the food and beverages he consumes become blood and tissue and energy; food that is not suitable (kosher) for a Jew can only alienate him from matters of *Yiddishkeit*, for only the proper kosher food can nourish him physically, mentally, and spiritually.

(From a letter of the Rebbe, dated the 15th of Av, 5735)

FAMILY PURITY

HEALTHY CHILDREN THROUGH OBSERVANCE OF MITZVOS, PARTICULARLY TAHARAS HAMISHPACHAH

To parents who asked the Rebbe's blessing for healthy children, the Rebbe replied:

... It is obvious that the said blessing of healthy offspring, both physically and spiritually, largely depends on the parents' conduct; just as the physical health and constitution of the parents has an impact on the physical health of the children, the same is true with regard to their mental and spiritual health.

Indeed, as every intelligent person understands, the spiritual aspect is stronger than the physical, so that the order should in fact be reversed, namely, that the spiritual impact is predominant.

... Human nature is such that parents will make every sacrifice for the benefit of their children. They will do so even when the benefits may not be certain — as long as it has a chance [of succeeding].

All the above is by way of introduction to my earnest plea that regardless of how you conducted yourself in the past, you will [from now on] strengthen your commitment and adherence to the Will of G-d, the Creator and Source of all blessings.

This is particularly so in the area of the strict fulfillment of the laws and regulations of family purity, which aside from the essential aspect — that they are Divine imperatives — also have the Divine promise of reward in terms of healthy offspring, physically, mentally and spiritually.

(From a letter of the Rebbe, dated the 7th of Menachem Av, 5740)

ENHANCED OBSERVANCE OF FAMILY PURITY
WILL ENHANCE CHILD'S HEALTH

... After asking your forgiveness, I must however state the truth, that in the majority of circumstances, such a thing about which you write, [i.e., your child's skin ailment,] results from the fact that at the time the mother became pregnant, the laws and regulations of family purity were not properly observed.

If, G-d forbid, this applies to you as well, this can be rectified and ameliorated to a certain extent by beginning now to observe the laws and regulations of family purity in the fullest possible measure and also to influence others to also observe the laws in like manner.

G-d, "Who sees into one's heart," seeing that you have made a firm resolution to do so, both with regard to yourself as well as influencing others, will transmit His success to the course of treatment that will be undertaken by the doctor so that your son will be healed to a very great degree — and when you will do the above to the fullest extent, [i.e., observe family purity,] he will be healed to the fullest extent as well.

Hopefully you will be able to find the appropriate words with which to explain the above to your wife as well, and may G-d will it that you be able to convey glad tidings regarding all the above.

It would also be most advisable for you to check your *tefillin* as well as the *mezuzos* in your home, to insure that they are kosher according to Jewish law, and to give *tzedakah* every weekday morning prior to prayers.

Your wife *tichyeh* should observe the "good custom" of upstanding Jewish women of giving *tzedakah* before lighting the candles every *erev Shabbos* and *erev Yom Tov*.

(Igros Kodesh, Vol. XVI, p. 357)

WELLNESS OF CHILD AND TAHARAS HAMISHPACHAH

... I received your note in which you write about your son:

If you inform me of your son's full Hebrew name as well as your full Hebrew name, I will remember him in prayer for a speedy recovery.

I trust you will not take offense at the following remarks, but I consider it my duty to mention that this kind of disorder in children is quite often due to the fact that the parents did not properly observe the laws of *Taharas HaMishpachah*, the laws of family purity, at the time of conception.

If — G-d forbid — this was indeed the case, bear in mind that *teshuvah* (repentance) is also effective retroactively to quite a great extent, so that it is possible to rectify the failures of the past.

You and your husband should firmly resolve to observe the laws of *Taharas HaMishpachah* from now on, and try to impress upon your friends as well the vital importance of observing these laws.

(From a letter of the Rebbe, dated the 27th of Shevat, 5721)

HEALTH OF NEWBORN CHILD
AND TAHARAS HAMISHPACHAH

One of the essential *mitzvos* is *Taharas HaMishpachah*, which, as explained in our holy sources, is directly related to the well-being of newborn children.

Although each of G-d's commandments must be observed for its own sake, G-d revealed to us that each *mitzvah* also has a unique significance of its own, connected to the spiritual and physical well-being of the person fulfilling the *mitzvah*.

Incidentally, the importance of this particular *mitzvah* [of *Taharas HaMishpachah* and *mikveh*] can also be gleaned from the fact that when our Sages of the *Mishnah* wish to illustrate how G-d provides us with a pure heart, they say, "Just as a *mikveh* purifies, so does the Holy One blessed be He."[9]

(From a letter of the Rebbe, dated the 21st of Menachem Av, 5724)

SPIRITUAL ASSISTANCE OF RELATIVES IN PROMOTING HEALING

THE SPIRITUAL ASSISTANCE OF PARENTS FOR THEIR AILING CHILD

In reply to your question as to how you can be of assistance to your [ill] daughter:

When parents conduct their daily life according to the desire — as delineated in the *Shulchan Aruch* — of G-d, the "Healer of all flesh and Performer of wonders,"[10] this increases the success of the treatment by the flesh-and-blood doctor (who is the agent of the "Healer of all flesh").

Even if the parents imagine that it is difficult for them to change their past manner of conduct, still, parents do even more difficult things for the sake of their children.

As to your traveling here [to see me] — there is absolutely no need to do so, for my response is [and will continue to be] as above. Rather, the cost of the journey should be given to *tzedakah* for the merit of your daughter *tichye*.

(From a letter of the Rebbe, dated the 25th of Tammuz, 5731)

---

9. *Yoma*, conclusion of the chapter entitled *Yom HaKippurim*.
10. Conclusion of *"Asher Yotzar"* blessing, from *Berachos* 60b.

IMPACT OF CHILDREN'S POSITIVE SPIRITUAL BEHAVIOR ON THE HEALTH OF THEIR PARENTS

I received your letter in which you write about the medical treatment your mother will be undergoing.

As requested, I will remember her again in prayer for the success of the medical treatment.

Needless to say, every additional effort in matters of Torah and *mitzvos* on your part, and also on the part of the other family members, will bring additional Divine blessings to all the family, and particularly to your mother.

The good conduct of a son is especially credited to his parents, and therefore stands them in good stead. [No matter how laudable your conduct has been until now,] in matters of goodness and holiness there is, of course, always room for improvement. ...

(From a letter of the Rebbe, dated the 3rd of Iyar, 5720)

ASSORTED SPIRITUAL ASSISTS TO HEALING

HEALING THROUGH JOY

I received your telegram about your daughter *tichye*'s [state of health] and today I received your letter from the 22nd of Kislev as well.

When I was at the holy resting place of my father-in-law, the Rebbe, of sainted memory, I mentioned your daughter in prayer for a speedy recovery. Surely you will not keep good news from me, and you will notify me [of your daughter's improved health] as soon as possible.

It is well known that "Joy breaks all boundaries."[11] It would therefore be proper for you and your family to participate — either personally or at least by assisting — in the preparations to the chassidic *farbrengens* that are held from time to time in your locale. This will also serve to hasten your daughter *tichye*'s recovery.

In the future, when you write about your daughter's healing, the language should be, as is known, "to all her bodily parts" and not "to her 248 bodily parts."

With blessing that you soon be able to convey glad tidings.

(Igros Kodesh, Vol. VII, p. 94)

DOING A FAVOR FOR A FELLOW JEW
A SPIRITUAL VESSEL TO RECEIVE G-D'S MANIFEST BLESSINGS

... One of the best ways to receive additional blessings from G-d is by doing a fellow Jew a favor, either materially or spiritually; just as one can always find an individual who is in need of material *tzedakah*, the same is true regarding doing a spiritual favor.

The more one occupies himself in this matter, the more one derives personal satisfaction from one's labors. [And] all this is in addition to performing a *mitzvah* of the Torah, namely, the commandment to "Love your fellow as yourself,"[12] concerning which Rabbi Akiva states:[13] "This is a primary principle of the Torah," — something that draws down additional blessings from G-d.

Such conduct has a direct or [at least an] indirect effect on the improvement of one's health, as well as in more accurately assessing all that is happening to oneself and around him. ...

(Igros Kodesh, Vol. XVIII, p. 138)

---

11. See *Sefer HaMaamarim 5657*, p. 223ff.
12. *Vayikra* 19:18.
13. *Yerushalmi*, *Nedarim* 9:4.

NO USE OF AMULETS

You write about [providing you with] an amulet [as a *segulah* for the improvement of your health]:

This is not our approach or custom. Strengthening your *bitachon* in G-d, "Healer of all flesh, and Performer of wonders,"[14] is one of the best spiritual *segulos*.

(From a letter of the Rebbe, dated the 24th of Cheshvan, 5728)

In another letter[15] where the writer asks about amulets, the Rebbe responded:

"I have heard nothing at all about [employing] such matters."

FORSAKE PATH OF SEGULOS
EXCEPT FOR "SEGULAH" OF TORAH AND MITZVOS

You write that you saw in a book a *segulah* or something similar [that will bring about healing]:[16]

Forsake the path of *segulos*, as people and circumstances tend to differ, [and] not everyone possesses the knowledge and ability to perceive and unmistakably know the ins and outs of these matters.

[So why use the path of *segulos* at all] when there exists the tried and proven "*segulah*" of following the path of Torah and *mitzvos* — as I have already written to you in my previous letters.

May the "Healer of all flesh and Performer of wonders" enlighten you regarding all the above and grant a full and speedy recovery to your mother *shetlita*.

(*Igros Kodesh*, Vol. XIV, p. 394)

---

14. From the text of the "*Asher Yatzar*" blessing, from *Berachos* 60b.
15. *Igros Kodesh*, Vol. XX, p. 119.
16. In this case, writing the words *Kra Satan* ("obliterate *Satan*") on a piece of parchment.

NO TO SEGULOS —
YES TO CHECKING MEZUZOS AND RECITING TEHILLIM

You ask that I provide you with a *segulah* [for increased good health]:

It is not my approach to provide *segulos*; however, as in all Jewish homes, the *mezuzos* are to be checked. Also see to it that the one in need of [increased good health] recite *Tehillim* daily.

(*Igros Kodesh*, Vol. IV, p. 247)

CHECKING MEZUZOS, TEFILLIN, AND GIVING TZEDAKAH

To an individual who was suffering from acute anxiety, the Rebbe advised:

I would also suggest that you have the *mezuzos* of your home checked as well as your *tefillin*, and that before putting on your *tefillin* every weekday morning, you put aside a small coin for *tzedakah*.

(From a letter of the Rebbe, dated the 26th of Teves, 5725)

SPIRITUAL ASSISTS FOR HEALTH

To a woman who was having health problems, the Rebbe wrote:

It would be well to have your *mezuzos* checked to make sure they are kosher and properly affixed. Also, you are no doubt aware of and observe the "good custom" — *bli neder* — of putting aside a coin for *tzedakah* before lighting the candles [on *erev Shabbos* and *erev Yom Tov*].

(From a letter of the Rebbe, dated the 21st of Kislev, 5733)

TEHILLIM, TZEDAKAH AND PARTAKING IN
PUBLIC TORAH STUDY AS VEHICLES FOR HEALING

I was informed by ... that you are unwell and that you ask for a blessing:

Surely you are under the care of a good doctor and you are following his instructions, as G-d always desires that things should come about through an agent who exists within the natural realm and that the healing come about in a natural way.

One needs however to make a [spiritual] vessel through which G-d's desire [that you be healed] will come to pass. The vehicle for this is to recite several chapters of *Tehillim* daily, to give *tzedakah* according to your ability, and to participate in a public Torah study session that is given in the synagogue.

I hope you will begin doing these things as quickly as possible. ...

(Igros Kodesh, Vol. IV, p. 41)

SATISFACTION FELT WHEN DOING GOOD DEEDS STRENGTHENS NOT ONLY SPIRITUAL HEALTH, BUT PHYSICAL HEALTH AS WELL

... Of course one must obey the instructions of the doctor when he says that you must take care of your health, and indeed, this is the Torah command,[17] "Scrupulously guard your health." However, when G-d inscribed this in His Torah, He concurrently wrote about the importance of performing deeds of righteousness and kindness (*tzedakah v'chessed*).

Surely, then, it is possible to act in this manner [of performing deeds of righteousness and kindness] where not only will this not harm your health, but on the contrary [it will improve it,] for the satisfaction and pleasure felt when doing a good deed strengthens and enhances [not only a Jew's spiritual health, but also] a Jew's physical health.

The same is true with regard to your situation [and your difficulties in speaking loudly]: even if you will not speak loudly, people will surely be able to hear what you are saying. ...

(Igros Kodesh, Vol. X, p. 50)

---

17. *Devarim* 4:15.

ALL-ENCOMPASSING PRAYER OF HEALTH

Attention can be called to our Sages' statement (*Megillah* 17b, explained in the *Tzemach Tzedek's* commentary to *Tehillim* 6:1) that [requests for] healing are mentioned in the eighth blessing [of the *Shemoneh Esreh*], the blessing *Refa'einu*, where we ask: "Grant complete cure and healing... ."

An association can be made with the eighth candle, [i.e., my father-in-law, the Rebbe, the eighth Rebbe,] (in the chain of leaders of the chassidic movement: the Baal Shem Tov, the Maggid of Mezritch,...), [and the eighth Rebbe,] Yosef ([who is associated with] the eighth king, Hadar,[18] as explained in the *Hosafos* to *Torah Or, Parshas Vayechi,* [and identified with] the level of *tzaddik*, the foundation of the world, and circumcision which is carried out on the eighth day. [Similarly,] Shemini Atzeres[19] is connected to Yosef — *Zohar* I, p. 208b; *Likkutei Torah* from the Rebbe Maharash, p. 71d).[20]

[So, too, regarding the Rebbe's second name] Yitzchak (which is numerically equivalent [208] to eight times the numerical equivalent of G-d's name *Y-H-V-H*,[21] as stated by the *Tzemach Tzedek* in *Or HaTorah, Bereishis,* p. 304a).

[This also relates to the] all-encompassing healing that will come in the Ultimate Future (see the *maamar* entitled *Samchuni* in the *Tzemach Tzedek's Derech Emunah*), in the era of *Mashiach*; may he come speedily in our days.

Then there will be a harp of eight strands and we will specifically say to Yitzchak: "For you are our father."[22] See (*Sanhedrin* 94a [which states]): "The Holy One, blessed be He, sought to make Chizkiyahu *Mashiach*."

---

18. See *Bereishis* 36:39.
19. The eighth day of the Sukkos holiday.
20. Reprinted in *Or HaTorah, Bereishis,* Vol. VI, p. 1065a.
21. The numerical equivalent of G-d's name *Y-H-V-H* is 26, and 8x26 equals 208.
22. *Shabbos* 89b.

[The passage continues, stating that *Mashiach* will not come] "until [the Jewish people] are repeatedly humiliated" (which has been fulfilled in the present era). [And it speaks of] Chizkiyahu as having eight names.

(*Igros Kodesh*, Vol. II, p. 27)

CHAPTER 9

Consulting
With a Specialist

A SPECIALIST IN THE PARTICULAR AILMENT SHOULD
SERVE AS THE PRIMARY CONSULTANT

I was somewhat taken aback about your writing that you are consulting with a doctor who is not a specialist [in your son's ailment,] but is an internist.

Although it has already been stated: "Salvation lies in much counsel,"[1] [i.e., it is of benefit to seek the counsel of more than one doctor,] nevertheless, it is readily understandable that the primary counsel emanate from a specialist in the particular area [of your son's illness]. And there are quite a number of such specialists in *Eretz Yisrael*.

[Moreover,] if the above applies in all instances of healing, how much more so when we are dealing with healing with a new drug, since, generally speaking, newly discovered drugs require much greater caution, as experience has shown.

(Igros Kodesh, Vol. XVII, p. 55)

SEEK OUT A SPECIALIST WITH MUCH EXPERIENCE

... With regard to [seeking] treatment for your face:

Seeking treatment is the correct course of action, for we have been commanded to do all that we can through natural means, and "Permission was granted the healer to heal."

---

1.   *Mishlei* 11:14.

However, you should seek out a doctor who is a specialist in this field, and more importantly, one who has had much experience in this area and who therefore will be able to more easily diagnose the exact type of treatment you are in need of. ...

(*Igros Kodesh*, Vol. XIX, p. 46)

EVEN WHEN THE DETERIORATION IN HEALTH IS ONLY TEMPORARY, TURN TO A SPECIALIST

Without a shadow of a doubt, your present [health] situation is only temporary.

However, in order to hasten this [healing], and since a person should do whatever he can in a natural manner, you should turn to a specialist in this area (according to the choice of a doctor [whom you also consider a] friend), and may G-d grant you success.

[Additionally,] increasing your *bitachon* in G-d will increase His blessings.

I will mention you in prayer at the holy resting place of my father-in-law, the Rebbe, of blessed memory, for good health.

(From a response of the Rebbe in 5732)

WHEN THERE IS DIFFICULTY IN DETERMINING A DIAGNOSIS, SEEK OUT THE GREATEST SPECIALIST IN THE FIELD

This is in reply to your letter, in which you write about the state of your health and summarize the condition of your ailment from the past few years, together with the treatment, etc., that you have received in the past:

It is not clear from your letter — although in all probability you have done so — whether you have inquired of the more prominent doctors in this field; many of whom are in Europe. Regarding an ailment such as you describe, particularly as there are uncertainties about it, it is worthwhile for you to communicate specifically with a renowned specialist.

On the other hand, it is not clear to me how doctors have failed until now to determine the cause of your disorder, what exactly ails you, and how to treat the ailment; after all, this has been going on — as it seems from your letter — for many years, [and] surely many X-rays have already been taken.

Clearly, my intent is not to bombard you with questions but to suggest to you that it would presently be worthwhile for you to find out who is the greatest specialist in this field, to send him the letters of the previous doctors who have treated you, as well as all the information he needs to know, and seek his general advice. Also, ask him whether it would be of benefit to you to see him.

May it be G-d's will, the "Healer of all flesh and Performer of wonders," that you obtain a speedy recovery through the right doctor and appropriate treatment. After all, is there anything that G-d cannot do?

(*Igros Kodesh*, Vol. XXII, p. 217)

TWO SPECIALISTS

I received through ... a *pidyon nefesh* for you, in which he writes that your health is not as it should be because of your gall bladder problems, and that doctors are advising you to have surgery.

No doubt you can obtain the opinion of two specialists in this field. May G-d help them to arrive at the correct diagnosis and be good emissaries so that you will be healed through them.

(*Igros Kodesh*, Vol. VI, p. 218)

FOLLOW THE INSTRUCTIONS OF THE DOCTOR
WHO PROVIDED THE MORE ACCURATE DIAGNOSIS

... Consult with the doctor whose diagnosis was more accurate than that provided by the first doctor you visited (for which reason it is advisable to follow [the second doctor's] instructions).

(Igros Kodesh, Vol. XIII, p. 416)

SEEK OUT THE ADVICE OF A SPECIALIST

... Since G-d desires that we do everything we can in a natural manner, it is important that you receive the advice of an expert — in your situation a doctor who specializes in nervous and mental conditions — and follow his advice.

(Igros Kodesh, Vol. XX, p. 98)

REVISITING A DISTINGUISHED PHYSICIAN
WITH WHOM ONE WAS DISSATISFIED MANY YEARS BEFORE

... You write about Mr. ... *sheyichye*, that since he already visited Professor ... once before and was not satisfied at that time from the course of treatment he received, he therefore wants to wait until he hears my opinion once again as to whether I still maintain that he visit him, or whether I have changed my position:

... Many years have passed since he was unhappy with the results of his treatment at the hands of Professor... . I know, however, of many individuals who have turned to him for help and he has successfully treated them. I do not see why this should not be so in his case as well. ...

(Igros Kodesh, Vol. XXI, p. 213)

AGREEMENT OF AT LEAST TWO DOCTORS

With regard to your medical treatment: Do so according to the unanimous opinion of (at least) two specialists.

(Igros Kodesh, Vol. XXIV, p. 357)

CONSULT WITH THREE DOCTORS
ONE OF WHOM IS A FRIEND

... Consult about the above with three doctors — two of whom are specialists in *this particular field*, while the third should be a doctor who is also a friend, [even if he is not a specialist in the particular field].

Afterwards, either decide [the course of action] by yourself, or (should you be in doubt) with a *Rav* who *regularly* rules on Jewish law, ascertaining his ruling according to the *Shulchan Aruch*.

(From a letter of the Rebbe, in the year 5730)

WHEN IN DOUBT
SEEK THE ADVICE OF TWO SPECIALISTS

... With regard to the question of your and your mother's health:

As in all questions of health, if there is any doubt, one should act on the unanimous advice of at least two specialists.

(From a letter of the Rebbe, dated the 22nd of Adar I, 5725)

WHEN THE OPINION OF TWO DOCTORS CONFLICT
A THIRD DOCTOR SHOULD DECIDE BETWEEN THE TWO

In reply to your letter of the 29th of Sivan, [in which you write about the problem you are having] with your tooth:

Since you have been feeling pain for a considerable amount of time, it would indicate that things aren't as they should be. You should therefore take care of the situation and not neglect it [any longer].

If — as you write — there are differing opinions between the [two] doctors [as to the method of treatment], seek out the opinion of a third doctor who will advise you which of the two opinions you should follow.

(*Likkutei Sichos*, Vol. XXXVI, p. 318)

CONSULT WITH TWO SPECIALISTS
EXPLAIN TO THEM YOUR REASONING —
THEN FOLLOW THEIR INSTRUCTIONS

In reply to your letters ... in which you write about your health situation and the opinion of many of the doctors whose advice you sought...:

It would be appropriate that sometime during the month of Elul, the "Month of Mercy," a consultation take place between you and two of the specialists whom you have visited. Provide them with your reasons and then follow their instructions, for "Permission was granted a healer to heal."

(Igros Kodesh, Vol. XV, p. 293)

WHEN THE DOCTOR SUGGESTS NO TREATMENT AT ALL

With regard to your mother-in-law *tichye*:

The general rule in such matters is that if a doctor advises against any form of treatment, another specialist in this field should be consulted. It would therefore be worthwhile that your mother-in-law *tichye* also go to another specialist. ...

(Likkutei Sichos, Vol. XXXVI, p. 278[2])

---

2.   From a letter of the Rebbe, dated 14 Sivan, 5718.

CHAPTER 10

Obtaining a Second Opinion
And What to Do
When Doctors' Opinions Differ

WHEN TO SEEK THE COUNSEL
OF A GENERAL PRACTITIONER

I received your letter of the 27th of MarCheshvan in which you describe the health status of your wife *tichye*. According to her present doctor, she is suffering from any number of health problems. [You also write that] from time to time she has gall bladder attacks and is presently bedridden because of various pains:

In my opinion, it would be worthwhile to find a general practitioner, i.e., someone who may not be so renowned but has knowledge of all these ailments. Share with him the opinions of all the doctors who treated your wife until now.

Ask this doctor to get involved in [her case] and to provide her with a specific diet and general instructions on how to improve her health.

Since our Sages, of blessed memory, have stated that healing comes through "a specific medication and a particular healer," etc., without [his ability to succeed in healing] being limited to his greatness and renown, it is quite possible that specifically such a doctor will figure out exactly what ails her and that her healing will come about through him.

With blessings that you be able to relate glad tidings to me about the improvement of your wife *tichye*'s health.

(*Igros Kodesh*, Vol. V, p. 50)

WHEN THE OPINIONS OF DOCTORS DIFFER

With regard to that which you write about your health [and the differing opinions of the doctors as to which course of action to follow]:

In a situation where there is — such as you write — disagreement between doctors, you should make a consultation with three doctors and follow the opinion of the majority.

May G-d will it that [in the medical advice you receive] there be fulfilled the blessing of,[1] "G-d will bless you in all that you do."

(*Igros Kodesh*, Vol. XXIV, p. 185)

HESITATION ABOUT RECEIVING CONFLICTING MEDICAL ADVICE

... This is in regard to your question at the conclusion of your letter, whether you should see a more expert doctor than Dr. .... . You are hesitant about doing so as the new doctor may have a different opinion from the first, and then you would not know how to decide:

Even if this difference of opinion should arise — something that you cannot possibly know at present — you can then deal with it. [It should not, however, negate seeing a greater medical authority.]

[If there should be two opposite medical opinions,] the way to then deal with this situation is the following:

Either follow your instincts, for as the *Shulchan Aruch* rules that in medical matters the patient himself is sometimes the best judge; or present both opinions to a doctor who is neutral [and follow the objective opinion of the neutral doctor]. ...

(*Igros Kodesh*, Vol. X, p. 170)

---

1.   *Devarim* 15:18.

CONTINUE SEEING THE DOCTOR
WHOM YOU TRUST MOST

In response to your question [of which one of your former doctors you should now continue to see]:

Continue seeing the doctor in whom you place the most confidence and trust.

(Likkutei Sichos, Vol. XXXVI, p. 281[2])

FOLLOW THE OPINION OF MAJORITY OF DOCTORS —
IF THEY ALL DISAGREE, FOLLOW ADVICE OF FAMILY PHYSICIAN

With regard to your medical treatment:

Ask the opinion of a third specialist; if he agrees with the opinion of one [of the first two doctor's who are in disagreement,] then follow his advice.

If the specialist should offer a third opinion, then convey all this to your family doctor and consult with him as to what you should actually do.

(Ibid.[3])

WHEN DOCTORS' EGOS ARE INVOLVED

You write about ... *shetlita* and that they are consulting with two medical specialists without one specialist knowing that another is being consulted:

In order that there not be confusion later on, it would be appropriate that before they do anything, they diplomatically organize a meeting of these two specialists. ...

Understandably, if this will lead to anger and discontent on the part of [even] one of these doctors, then let it suffice that the

---

2.   From a letter of the Rebbe, dated *Motza'ei Shabbos*, 2nd day of *Rosh Chodesh Adar* I, 5733.

3.   *Ibid.*

two specialists voice their opinions before the family doctor and consult with him.

(Igros Kodesh, Vol. XIII, p. 220)

CHAPTER 11

Using Latest Techniques, Procedures and Medications

MEDICINE IN THE TALMUD

With regard to your question concerning the role of *Aggadah* in the *Talmud*, particularly those [passages] dealing with medicine:

... As to the question of medicine in the *Talmud*, [the various methods of healing, etc.,] are not at all as fantastic as they may appear. As a matter of fact, the therapeutic value of many medical suggestions in the *Talmud* have been confirmed in recent years, although medical science had long denied them.

Generally speaking, however, since the nature of the human organism has undergone many changes since those days, the medical advice contained in the *Talmud* cannot be applied nowadays. But it is quite certain that in their days the remedies were quite effective.

For references consult: *Tosafos, Moed Katan* 11a; *Kesef Mishnah*, ch. 4. of *Hilchos Deos*, law 18; and sources mentioned in *Sdei Chemed*, sec. of *Kelalim*, under "*Reish*" *Klal* 54, where it is stated that due to physical and climatic changes, medical treatment and remedies of old are no longer generally valid.

In the history of medical science, many examples are given regarding changes in man's susceptibility to disease and treatment, the development of virus attack, new diseases, etc. There is [already] quite an extensive body of literature on the subject, and [therefore] there is no need for me to [further] expand upon this subject.

(From a letter of the Rebbe, dated the 11th of Tishrei, 5712)

UTILIZING AND PUBLICIZING THE LATEST AND BEST
MEDICATIONS AND FORMS OF TREATMENT

I received your letter with the two attached articles, and as per your request, I reviewed your monograph. I must say that your explanation of how to avoid becoming resistant to medications is extremely sound.

It caused me to speculate why this method has not been accepted and used until now; although in the history of science there have been many similar occurrences, [i.e., where something that was scientifically and medically sound was nevertheless not picked up on].

Still, the past should instruct the future, and such occurrences [as failing to act on good science and medicine] should be on the decline.

Understandably, my intent is not to arouse speculation and doubt, but just to observe that it is possible that investigations have already been made in the direction that you suggest and that actions have already been taken along these lines, although surely you researched this matter to the greatest possible extent before you printed your article.

Parenthetically — although this is not my area of expertise:

I couldn't help notice that in the tables you use in your monograph you cite medications and methods that were in vogue over 150 years ago.

This also arouses wonder — for during this long period of time, these medications and methods were surely used on numerous occasions with changes and improvements made in the manner and means of use, treatment and administration.

It is impossible for there not to have been novel approaches either to the right or to the left, [i.e., that a medication or method of treatment came to be used more extensively or fell into disfavor].

Your intent in publishing the tables is not to record the history of medicine but to help obtain the maximum benefit regarding medications and their beneficial use. With regard to this matter [of the best use of medications, etc.,] one should use only the latest results.

This is also in keeping with the general principle of our Torah, which is also, *lehavdil*, a principle in logic that the law is in accordance with the opinions of those who lived later [*hilcheseh kibasra'i*], since they were also aware of the prior opinions [and nevertheless disagreed].

As is self-understood, this is only being written from the viewpoint of someone who is not writing in his area of expertise, just as a comment from someone who is on the outside. ...

(Igros Kodesh, Vol. XV, p. 351)

Assure That Latest Developed Medications And Forms of Treatment Are Being Utilized

... At an opportune time, I will mention Mrs. ... in prayer at the holy resting place of my father-in-law, the Rebbe, of blessed memory.

Surely she is under the care of a specialist. Try to find out whether they are using the medications and means of treatment that have recently been developed and which doctors are using with great success in the United States. No doubt the doctors in your country are aware of them as well.

It would be appropriate at this time to have her husband's *tefillin* checked, as well as to check the *mezuzos* in their home.

Also, she should give *tzedakah* prior to lighting candles *erev Shabbos* and *erev Yom Tov*.

(*Igros Kodesh*, Vol. XV, p. 114)

USING TREATMENTS AND MEDICATIONS
JUST OUT ON THE MARKET

... I am surprised that you do not mention the course of treatment suggested by the doctor. In a situation such as yours, many new treatments and medications have been developed in the past few years and [even] in the past few months. Among them are Ortisone and Cortisone and others.

Possibly [you are indeed being treated in the above manner, but] you merely failed to notify me about it. However, if this is not the case, [i.e., it is not merely a failure in notification,] then it would be good for you to ask [the doctor] specifically about this [matter of using the latest treatments and medications].

(*Igros Kodesh*, Vol. XV, p. 114)

INQUIRE ABOUT THE NEWEST METHODS
OF TREATMENT

At an opportune time, I will mention your son in prayer at the holy resting place of my father-in-law, the Rebbe, of blessed memory, for all that your son *shlita* requires, particularly regarding an improvement in those matters of his health about which you write, [i.e., his skin ailment].

Surely you will inquire of a specialist about the newest methods of treatment that have lately been discovered in this area, and whether they would be appropriate in the present circumstances.

(*Igros Kodesh*, Vol. XVI, p. 357)

MEDICAL ACHIEVEMENTS IN OTHER COUNTRIES

... With regard to the medical achievements of doctors in the United States:

Generally, the doctors in the United States and in *Eretz Yisroel* are in close contact and they are aware of one another's accomplishments in the field.

At times, however, it would be advantageous to ask your doctor specifically about the latest developments outside of *Eretz Yisroel* and particularly in the United States [since he may not be aware of them, as it may have not come up in his practice] — in keeping with the saying of our Sages, of blessed memory:[1] "People do not focus on matters they are not responsible for."

(*Igros Kodesh*, Vol. XX, p. 128)

---

1.   *Shevuos* 41b.

CHAPTER 12

Surgery and
Medical Procedures

WHEN DOCTORS DISAGREE
WHETHER SURGERY IS NECESSARY

... You write about the differing opinions among the doctors as to the correct course of treating your wife *tichye*, [with some of them suggesting surgery, while others do not]:

It is known that when there are doubts as to the wisdom of having surgery performed, then it is better not to have it performed.

May G-d, "Healer of all flesh and Performer of wonders," heal her and strengthen her in the proper manner and fulfil! your hearts' requests for the good.

(Igros Kodesh, Vol. XX, p. 88)

WHEN BEGINNING TO FEEL BETTER
SURGERY MAY BE UNNECESSARY

... I cannot definitively answer whether you should have surgery since your letter is not clear about what exactly ails you.

However, since you write in your letter that you are seeing an improvement in your health, hopefully you will get even better and surgery will be entirely unnecessary.

It would be advisable for you to ask the doctor who is treating you whether it would be worthwhile for you to go on a rice diet.

(Likkutei Sichos, Vol. XXXVI, p. 301[1])

---

1.   From a letter of the Rebbe, dated 9 Tammuz, 5725.

NEW AND COMPLEX SURGERY

The surgical procedure about which you write is: 1) very complex; 2) still in the developmental stages; [and] 3) few of these surgeries (in comparison to others at least) have been performed.

As a result, currently the effects of this form of surgery are not all that clear. Moreover — and this is of great import — the changes brought about by the surgery *cannot* be reversed.

Thus, if the situation is stable (i.e., it has not become any worse, G-d forbid) you should hold off on this surgery until much more is known than what is known about it [now].

(*Likkutei Sichos*, Vol. XXXVI, p. 301[2])

TIMING OF SURGERY

If another doctor concurs [that surgery is necessary], you should have it done in a good and auspicious time. Understandably — it is better [to have it done] in the month of Elul than in [the month of] Menachem Av.

In any event, the surgery should not be performed on Friday, but close to the beginning of the week.

(*Likkutei Sichos*, Vol. XXXVI, p. 301[3])

WITH THE AGREEMENT OF AT LEAST TWO DOCTORS

With regard to the medical procedure:

Act according to the concurring opinion of (at least) two specialists. (In any event, do not have [the procedure] performed during the Three Weeks, [i.e., between the Seventeenth of Tammuz and the Ninth of Av].)

(*Likkutei Sichos*, Vol. XXXVI, p. 301[4])

---

2.   From a reply of the Rebbe.
3.   *Ibid.*
4.   From a letter of the Rebbe, dated 5 Tammuz, 5727.

ELECTIVE SURGERY AND MEDICAL PROCEDURES
PRIOR TO SHABBOS

There are many medical procedures, particularly surgical operations, which, because of post-procedural recuperation and tests, require that a patient stay in the hospital after the actual procedure is completed.

It is customary in many countries, especially in the United States, to schedule such operations for Friday, and consequently, the recuperative period extends into *Shabbos*.

There are, however, several *halachic* considerations which cast serious doubt on the permissibility of such a procedure. We are not referring to emergency operations, for in cases of *pikuach nefesh*, when one's life is in danger, *Shabbos* assumes secondary status. We are referring to those operations and procedures that are scheduled well in advance.

The following are some of the reasons why operations, or other procedures warranting a stay in hospital, should not be scheduled for the second half of the week.

The *Shulchan Aruch,* the Jewish Code of Law, states (*Hilchos Shabbos* 248:1): "One should not [set] sail on a ship within three full days preceding *Shabbos;* that is, from Wednesday on, inclusive of Wednesday itself ... for on the first three days (of ocean travel) people are afflicted with pain and disturbances ... and they do not return to their original state until after three full days. Hence, if a person sails within three days preceding *Shabbos*, he will not enjoy *Shabbos*."

From this law it is clear that anything which creates disturbance and pain, or can mar one's enjoyment of *Shabbos* in general, must be avoided during the three days preceding *Shabbos*.

The disturbances one feels when entering a hospital, with its attendant changes in routine (in eating, sleeping, waking hours, even special clothes), and especially the pain and trauma that follows an operation, are much greater than those caused by sailing on a ship.

Moreover, unlike a sea voyage, the havoc wreaked on the enjoyment of *Shabbos* caused by a hospital stay affects one's family as well. Thus one should not enter a hospital from Wednesday on.

A further problem is that many of the post-operative procedures involve work that is forbidden on *Shabbos*. Although some of them may fall within the category of *pikuach nefesh*, necessary for the patient's essential welfare, one should not deliberately place himself in the position of having to desecrate the *Shabbos*.

In other words, one should not enter a hospital within three days of *Shabbos* knowing it will entail desecration of *Shabbos*.

This principle applies even if the forbidden tasks are performed by a non-Jew. The gravity of this situation is further compounded in cities where many of the hospital personnel may be Jewish (e.g., New York, Boston, etc.), and when the tests need the assistance of the patient.

Furthermore, even in many post-operative cases, the tests are not in the category of *pikuach nefesh* and must be deferred until after *Shabbos*.

A Jewish patient must then insist on having such tests performed after *Shabbos*; but immediately following an operation a patient does not usually have the requisite strength to refuse his doctors and insist on deferring the tests.

Moreover, many of these procedures are mandatory, not easily refused. And if one's attending physician is Jewish, the patient who enters the hospital on Friday is causing another Jew, the doctor, to desecrate the *Shabbos*.

All these factors lead to the conclusion that it is completely prohibited to arrange for a hospital procedure on Friday, or even Thursday or Wednesday. It is possible, and has been demonstrated so in the past, for one to arrange to enter a hospital at the beginning of the week.

A further point: Hospital shifts are so arranged that over the weekend (Saturday and Sunday) it is mainly interns who staff hospitals, and not the more experienced physicians.

Should some emergency arise, it is the more inexperienced doctor who will attend to it. Then, even from a purely medical view, it would be wise not to schedule surgery for Friday.

One more important point: If a person becomes sick, G-d forbid, Torah instructs us to seek the best medical assistance possible. Simultaneously however, a man must know that he is constantly being weighed on the Divine scale of good and bad.

An ill person would do well to consider that when his life or health is in danger, it is time to improve his conduct. His deeds must be beyond reproach, particularly in the very area of healing. In other words, the steps taken to become well (surgery, etc.) should be according to G-d's directives given to us in the Torah; then we may be sure that these steps will be successful.

Then G-d, the "Healer of all flesh and Performer of wonders," will bless each and every Jew with complete physical and spiritual health.

(*Likkutei Sichos*, Vol. XVI, p. 518ff.[5])

ELECTIVE SURGERY AND MEDICAL PROCEDURES ON FRIDAYS

... After asking your great forgiveness, I must however make you aware that a complex medical procedure or surgery should not take place on *erev Shabbos* — for any number of reasons:

As can be deduced from [the issues] of departing on a ship [on the second half of the week],[6] hospital procedures require that many tests be taken the day after the surgery, that matters be

---

5.   Excerpted from a talk on the second day of Shavuos, 5738.
6.   *Ibid.*

recorded and written down, etc. — some of them having no relationship at all to healing the individual, but merely for statistics and the like. In a city such as ... and similar cities, much of this is done by Jews, and many of them require the patients' assistance, and so on.

Moreover, and this too is of great importance: The present situation is that on *Shabbos* (and Sunday) it is mainly beginning interns who staff hospitals, and not the more experienced physicians, and there is quite a difference in the degree of expertise and competency between these two categories of physicians.

(*Likkutei Sichos*, Vol. XVI, p. 521[7])

USE OF THE WORD "TREATMENT" WITH REGARD TO SURGERY

... You ask me why I used the word "treatment" [with regard to your upcoming surgery]:

The reason is quite simple: I am referring to all the details in the treatment and healing process — that which transpires before surgery, that which transpires during surgery, and that which transpires during the recovery process following surgery. The purpose and intent of all these individual aspects is that they all lead to a speedy and full recovery. ...

(*Igros Kodesh*, Vol. XVIII, p. 267)

BEGIN WITH THE MOST BENIGN FORM OF TREATMENT

In reply to your letter of the 7th of Cheshvan where you write about the various suggestions offered by the doctors regarding assorted forms of treatment [in order for you to be able to bear children]:

Understandably, in such situations, [i.e., where there are a variety of options,] one is to begin with the easiest and most

---

7.   From a letter of the Rebbe, dated the first day of *Rosh Chodesh* Iyar, 5737.

uncomplicated [form of treatment,] i.e., merely soaking in the baths in Tiberius.

May G-d will it that the treatment meet with complete success, and may G-d very shortly fulfill your desire to have children.

(Igros Kodesh, Vol. XVIII, p. 50)

AVOID RADICAL TREATMENT
WHENEVER POSSIBLE

This is to acknowledge receipt of your letter of the 7th of Adar in which you write about the proposed surgery for Mrs. ... . I will remember her in prayer that whatever the final decision, it should meet with success.

Since you also ask my advice in this matter, I can only say that, in general, I am not in favor of radical treatment if there is any possibility in treating a patient in some other way.

I must also add that it is customary among Jews that when there is a difference of opinion among doctors as to the urgency of an operation, or whether or not to operate, it should be treated as any other question in Jewish law requiring consultation with a competent practicing *Rav*. The various aspects and details of the case should be explained to him, at which time he can state his opinion in accordance with the *Shulchan Aruch*.

I trust there is no need to emphasize at length that one always requires the blessings of the "Healer of all flesh and Performer of wonders." The channel to receive His blessings is through living one's everyday life in accordance with His Divine will, namely, in accordance with the Torah and *mitzvos*. When a special Divine blessing is needed, [then] an additional effort in this direction is called for.

(From a letter of the Rebbe, dated the 9th of Adar, 5739)

Undergoing Tests to Determine
The Cause of Feeling Weak

[This is] in reply to your letter, in which you inform me of the state of your health — that you are feeling weak and the doctor wants you to go for tests. You ask my opinion whether you should do so.

[My reply]: You may accede to his request and take the tests.

With regard to your feeling weak: Make sure that you eat in the morning, and that from time to time you learn something, whether in *Nigleh* or in *Chassidus*, from which you will derive clear-cut and actual physical pleasure. ...

(*Igros Kodesh*, Vol. XXI, p. 120)

Avoid Tests That Will Be of No Value
Even if They Are Relatively Benign

I received your special delivery letter in which you describe your daughter *tichye*'s visit to the doctor and that the doctor suggested a variety of tests in order to ascertain which category she belongs to, and you also describe the various categories.

From the tenor of your writing, it would seem that the doctor caused you to be heavyhearted and you ask my opinion about [your daughter] having these tests:

In my opinion I don't see how the test results — whatever they will show — will in any way affect your daughter's development. Since they will be of no value, then no matter how benign these tests may be, still, since these tests are performed through the use of electricity near the head and the like, it is difficult to predict whether these tests will in some way prove harmful.

Such tests are to be taken only when absolutely necessary, particularly since these tests are not yet of proven benefit as it is only a few years since these tests have been developed and doctors are still half in the dark about them.

You should also take into consideration that you yourself observed that the doctors' diagnosis about your daughter was flawed, and a greater degree of improvement has taken place than they originally thought possible. Surely this degree of improvement will continue in the future as well.

I therefore see no reason why you should lose money and put any undue strain on yourself with regard to tests that will provide no benefit, and that will, at best, cause no harm. ...

(Igros Kodesh, Vol. VI, p. 115)

ADDITIONAL DANGEROUS MEDICAL TESTS

... I am not pleased by the suggestion that your son ... *sheyichye* be subjected to additional medical tests that are extremely dangerous.

May G-d grant that even without these [additional] tests the doctors be able to establish a proper course of treatment and healing for him. May there be fulfilled through [the doctors] the saying of our Sages, of blessed memory: "Permission was granted — which also means that they were empowered — to the healer to heal."

Although [in general] one should follow the instructions of doctors, [they should] not [be followed] in this case where the tests are extremely dangerous.

(Likkutei Sichos, Vol. XXXVI, p. 302[8])

---

8.   From a letter of the Rebbe, dated 7 Menachem Av, 5712.

TREATMENTS AND PROCEDURES TO ACHIEVE PREGNANCY
SHOULD BEGIN WITH THE MOST UNCOMPLICATED AND BENIGN

In reply to your letter of the 16th of Menachem Av [5710] in which you describe the state of your wife *tichye's* health:

It is hard to understand that which you write concerning the reasons why your wife cannot conceive, when in the beginning of the letter you write that in Elul, 5709 she did become pregnant. [If she could conceive then,] surely she should be able to conceive now as well.

It therefore seems to me that she should not take — to quote you — "extreme measures." Rather she should again inquire of a specialist what she should do; surely he will find more benign methods of treatment.

Through "this specific doctor and this particular medication," everything will surely turn out well, and the blessing of my father-in-law, the Rebbe, הכ״מ — that G-d should cause your hearts to rejoice with viable and healthy children — will be fulfilled.

(*Igros Kodesh*, Vol. III, p. 386)

FOLLOW ADVICE OF SPECIALISTS
WHO RECOMMEND SURGERY

In reply to your letter ... in which you cite the opinion of the specialists whom you have recently visited regarding how you should be treated for your ailment [and their recommendation of surgery]:

Our Torah, the Torah of Life, grants permission for physicians to heal, and this empowers them to be instruments of healing as well, [for which reason you should follow their recommendation].

May G-d will it that your surgery lead to a rapid healing and a complete recovery. ...

(*Igros Kodesh*, Vol. XIX, p. 3)

Consult With At Least Two — Better Yet Three — Specialists Prior to Surgery

In reply to your letter of the first day of Chanukah in which you write about surgery for removal of a gland, etc.:

As in all matters of surgery, i.e., an act that cannot be undone, you should ask the opinion of experts in the field; at least two, and even better three.

I am sure that your father-in-law *sheyichye* will not oppose this, for even according to the directives of our Torah, the Torah of Life, the opinion of two or three individuals carries with it much more force than does the opinion of a solitary individual.

Rational human thought concurs with this as well, for any one individual, no matter who he is, is a created and inherently limited being. When there is a consultation among two or three individuals together, the result is that in "Salvation lies in much counsel."[9]

(*Igros Kodesh*, Vol. XVI, p. 183)

Radiation or Surgery

In reply to your letter of the 19th of Cheshvan, [where you write] about your health situation and the [different] opinions of the doctors [as to whether you should have surgery or radiation]:

Generally speaking, from the two alternatives you mention, surgery or radiation, you should lean towards the former — understandably after having received the consent of a Rabbi who regularly rules on matters of Jewish law.

[The reason for my opinion is] that one can never predict the outcome of the radiation with certainty, i.e., whether one has accomplished what one is seeking to accomplish, [that is to say, whether the tumor has been wholly and successfully irradiated].

---

9. *Mishlei* 11:14.

As is customary in such matters, you should have a concurring opinion of two specialists in the field, in addition to the agreement of the Rabbi, as previously mentioned.

May G-d lead you in the pathway that is best for you in all aspects.

You observe no doubt the "good custom" of Jewish women to always give *tzedakah* prior to lighting candles *erev Shabbos* and *erev Yom Tov*.

(*Igros Kodesh*, Vol. XXII, p. 354)

RECEIVE TWO CONCURRING OPINIONS
BEFORE UNDERGOING A PROCEDURE

[This is] in reply to your letter of the 17th of Teves ... in which you write about your health and the opinion of the doctor [that you should have a procedure done]:

In response to your question in this matter: You should act in accordance with the concurring opinion of two doctors.

Additionally — and of greatest import — place your *bitachon* in G-d, "Healer of all flesh and Performer of wonders,"[10] that the procedure be successful.

May you have a speedy healing.

(*Igros Kodesh*, Vol. XXIV, p. 50)

AFTER FIVE YEARS OF REGULAR TREATMENT,
WHY SUDDENLY OPERATE?

In reply to your question [whether your wife should immediately have surgery]:

Since your wife *tichye* has already been undergoing treatment for more than five years, why suddenly operate? In any event,

---

10.   From the text of the *"Asher Yatzar"* blessing, from *Berachos* 60b.

[you should] consult and follow the unanimous advice of three specialists.

It would be proper for you to check your *tefillin* and *mezuzos* to assure that they are kosher according to Jewish law.

Most importantly, strengthen your daily conduct so that it be in keeping with the directives of our Torah, the Torah of Life, and the performance of its commandments concerning which it is stated,[11] "You shall live by them."

In addition to the main point that [one should do so because] G-d has so commanded, this is also the path through which one receives G-d's blessings regarding all those things that a person needs.

(From a letter of the Rebbe, dated the 19th of Sivan, 5730)

DIET AND TRANQUILITY PREFERABLE TO SURGERY

In reply to your letter ... in which you describe your health status and the opinion of the doctor:

Since the doctor says that if you continue your diet you can forgo surgery for at least a year or two, then it is understandable that there is no room for thinking about undergoing surgery, particularly since from time to time new methods are discovered to treat a situation such as yours. Thus it is quite possible that you will not require surgery at all.

The matter depends on your self-control — not to become upset and angry, to more or less stick to your diet, and in general to follow the instructions of your specialist. ...

(*Igros Kodesh*, Vol. XIV, p. 151)

---

11. *Vayikra* 18:5.

FOLLOW ADVICE OF SPECIALISTS
WHO RECOMMEND SURGERY

In reply to your letter ... in which you cite the opinion of the specialists whom you have recently visited regarding how you should be treated for your ailment [and their recommendation of surgery]:

Our Torah, the Torah of Life, grants permission for physicians to heal, and this empowers them to be agents of healing as well, [for which reason you should follow their recommendation].

May G-d will it that your surgery lead to a rapid healing and a complete recovery. ...

(Igros Kodesh, Vol. XIX, p. 3)

TRY TO REFRAIN FROM EMPLOYING MEASURES
THAT CANNOT BE UNDONE

In light of the rapid advances in medical research during the past few years, every new day carries the possibility of bringing with it new medical knowledge and revelations.

A person should therefore seek to refrain from employing measures that cannot be undone when the new medical techniques and knowledge will have discovered that the original measures should not have been taken. ...

(Igros *Kodesh,* Vol. XIX, p. 134)

INQUIRE OF A RABBI WHO REGULARLY ISSUES HALACHIC RULINGS
PRIOR TO HAVING HALACHICALLY QUESTIONABLE SURGERY

With regard to the question in your letter about having the procedure done (the operation, etc.) [for purposes of fertility]:

Before anything else, you must ascertain from a practicing *Rav* whether this operation is permissible according to the Torah, the Torah of Life.

(Igros Kodesh, Vol. XXIV, p. 208)

AVOID THE PROCEDURE
DURING THE "THREE WEEKS"

With regard to your medical treatment: ... In any event do not undergo the procedure during the "Three Weeks," [i.e., between the Seventeenth of Tammuz and the Ninth of Av].

(Igros Kodesh, Vol. XXIV, p. 357)

SURGERY DURING THE NINE DAYS
AND CLOSE TO SHABBOS

...Your desire to do the above, [i.e., to have your operation] in the "Nine Days" [between *Rosh Chodesh* Menachem Av and Tishah BeAv,] and close to *Shabbos*, is not at all understandable.

It would be advisable to push off the surgery to [a day at] the beginning of the week, and after Tishah BeAv.

(From a letter of the Rebbe, dated Rosh Chodesh Menachem Av, 5731)

DELAY SURGERY UNTIL AFTER TISHAH BEAV

In reply to your question transmitted to me by ... with regard to your health status and the opinion of the doctor:

In general, one should act in accordance with the instructions of two specialists in the field, [and] since you write that both of them are in agreement, you should therefore undergo the procedure.

With regard to the timing:

If at all possible, try to push it off until after the ninth day [of Av, i.e., Tishah BeAv,] and if the doctor insists that the procedure be performed at an earlier date, then do it prior to *Shabbos Chazon.*

May G-d, "Healer of all flesh and Performer of wonders,"[12] send His "healing words" and heal you through [the medium of]

---

12. From the text of the "*Asher Yatzar*" blessing, from *Berachos* 60b.

"this specific doctor and this particular medication." And may you be able to convey glad tidings of openly revealed goodness.

(Igros Kodesh, Vol. XIX, p. 376)

FOLLOW DOCTOR'S ADVICE OF DIET, RATHER THAN SURGERY

... With regard to your friend [who faces the possibility of surgery]:

Since one of the doctors says that surgery is unnecessary and he need only be careful about his diet, he should follow that doctor's advice.

Your friend should also strengthen his *bitachon* in G-d, the "Healer of all flesh and Performer of wonders," [particularly since] peace of mind is one of the most potent cures for ailments such as your friend is suffering.

(Igros Kodesh, Vol. IX, p. 235)

CHAPTER 13

Ambulances, Hospitals,
And the Hospital Stay

AMBULANCE SERVICE

In conjunction with the benefit *Melavah Malkah* that is being held this Saturday night on behalf of [the Jewish ambulance service,] *Hatzolah,* now is the proper time to say a few words about it:

As we still find ourselves in exile, [a time when illness is existent,] ... we still need to approach healing through natural means, as the verse states:[1] "And he shall heal," [i.e., the doctor is thus G-d's agent to bring about healing].[2]

However, here as well (i.e., during times of exile), there are, as is known, two forms of healing: a) after one already became ill, Heaven forbid, he requires the assistance of a doctor and medications to heal him; b) before ever becoming ill, the person takes preventive measures so that he will not become ill in the first place.

This latter form of healing reflects G-d's form of healing, which is described in the verse[3] as being in a manner of, "No illness shall befall you, for I am G-d your healer." Something along these lines can also be accomplished by human beings, as the *Rambam* states in *Hilchos Deos*[4] — after describing how a person

---

1. *Shemos* 21:19.
2. See *Berachos* 60a and additional sources cited there.
3. *Shemos* 15:26. See also commentary of *Rashi* there.
4. 4:20.

should conduct himself in order to stay healthy — "Whoever conducts himself accordingly, I guarantee him that he will never fall ill ... he will not require a doctor."

We may well say that in a more sophisticated sense, this [form of preventive healing] also can result from knowing and reflecting about the very existence of healing and healers:

When a person is aware of the existence of healing and healers, this itself brings him some degree of tranquility and peace of mind, thereby assisting him in becoming well. At times it can even act as a means to remain healthy [in which case the person won't even] have to face a situation where healing becomes a necessity.

Accordingly, we may say that this very fact (that knowing about the existence of healing, doctors, and medications helps a person prevent illness) is accomplished to an even greater extent by knowing of the existence of *Hatzolah*:

Even if a person is aware of the existence of healers and medications, since they are not in close proximity to him, he may still lack utter tranquility and peace of mind. When, however, he is aware that a *Hatzolah* ambulance is immediately available and will quickly take him to the physician and healing medications, this in itself will cause him to be calm and serene.

Thereby he will avoid the necessity of ever being in need of an ambulance, knowing as he does that should he ever require one, it will be readily available.

In addition to the above: When a person goes outside and sees a *Hatzolah* ambulance before his eyes, it serves as an appropriate reminder to obey the instructions of his doctor, who was permitted and empowered by the Torah to heal. He will remember that the doctor told him time and again how he should protect his health, to eat healthily and not be a glutton, etc.

When the person sees the ambulance before him, he realizes that if he does not conduct himself in a healthful manner, he may be in need of the services of this very *Hatzolah* ambulance. This itself assures that he will never have to deal with a situation where it becomes necessary to use the *Hatzolah* ambulance.

(Likkutei Sichos, Vol. XXVI, p. 392[5])

HOSPITALS

HEALTH RISKS UNIQUE TO HOSPITAL

... I am usually very reluctant to express my view on matters that lie outside my field of competence. However, having glanced through the detailed research program that you enclosed in your letter I decided to share an observation [with you]:

I fail to find among the itemized points of study one aspect which, in my humble opinion, should have been of particular interest.

I am referring to the recognition that certain microbes and infections may be particularly linked to hospitals — a view which, I believe, has received some attention in pertinent literature.

I am not familiar with the details of this problem, but I believe it has to do with the ability of bacteria to develop immunity to antibiotics, as has been established in the case of penicillin, etc.

Hence, it is very possible that methods of infection control that are effective elsewhere may lose their effectiveness because of their continued and consistent application in hospitals, [causing the bacteria to become immune to this form of infection control,] or because the hospital environment has produced certain strains

---

5. From a *sichah* of the Rebbe, dated *Shabbos Parshas Pikudei, Parshas Shekalim, Mevarchim HaChodesh v'erev Rosh Chodesh* Adar Sheni, 5744.

of certain bacteria, which has given them a measure of immunity in that specific environment. ...

I do not know whether the omission of this aspect from your project is due to the fact that a three-month study period would not be sufficient to include an investigation into this area, since, undoubtedly, it would entail the problem of distinguishing "immunized" from "non-immunized" bacteria, etc., as well as the problems of changing methods of sterilization and infection control and clinical observation, etc. Or, simply, because this question is outside your present work.

Yet, it seems to me that this is a question of practical importance and should be well within your field of interest.

(From a letter of the Rebbe, dated *erev* Lag BaOmer, 5729)

THE HOSPITAL STAY

TAKE ALONG A MEZUZAH FOR YOUR HOSPITAL DELIVERY

I received your letter of November 12th in which you inform me that you expect to enter the hospital on Tuesday the 20th (tomorrow).

I pray and trust that everything will be well, and that you will soon be able to send me the joyous news [about the birth of a child].

I would suggest that you have with you at the hospital a kosher *mezuzah*, which should be kept in an envelope within an envelope and wrapped in an oilcloth (or other waterproof cloth). Keep this as near to you as possible, viz., under your pillow or in the table by your bedside, until you leave the hospital.

... It would be a good thing if you would take upon yourself, jointly with your husband, to contribute (without making a pledge

— *bli neder*) to kosher charities an amount equal to the cost of the delivery. ...

I wish you a good delivery and a normal and healthy offspring, and am looking forward to [hearing] good news of the happy event.

(From a letter of the Rebbe, dated the 20th of Cheshvan, 5712)

A MEZUZAH IN THE HOSPITAL ROOM

... May G-d help you that the operation be successful and that you be able to convey glad tidings about this.

It would be good if you could have a *mezuzah* with you in your hospital room. Also, [you should] undertake that as soon as you leave the hospital, you will give some *tzedakah* for the charity of R. Meir Baal HaNes prior to candle lighting *erev Shabbos* and *erev Yom Tov*.

Additionally, you should undertake to recite a chapter of *Tehillim* in Hebrew daily — if this is difficult for you, then [you can recite it] in English. ...

(*Likkutei Sichos*, Vol. XXXI, p. 264[6])

ALLEVIATING AGITATION DURING A HOSPITAL STAY[7]

Bring him a *Tanya* and have him read it occasionally; also [bring him] a (checked) *mezuzah*, placed in an envelope within an envelope.

(*Likkutei Sichos*, Vol. XXXVI, p. 299[8])

---

6. From a letter of the Rebbe, dated 26 Nissan, 5746.
7. Written to an individual whose father was extremely agitated during his hospital stay.
8. From a reply of the Rebbe.

VITAL IMPORTANCE OF DONNING TEFILLIN
DURING A HOSPITAL STAY

I duly received the *pidyon nefesh* on behalf of Mr. ...; surely he took along his *tefillin* [for his hospital stay,] and surely you also gave him the [printed] "Message" from my father-in-law, the Rebbe, of blessed memory.

Make sure to exhort him time and again that he put on *tefillin* daily — except understandably on *Shabbos* and *Yom Tov*. If he cannot do so in the morning, then he should put them on sometime during the day, until sunset; he should do so at least for a brief period of time, although he may have to remove his *tefillin* immediately after putting them on.

Explain to him that this *mitzvah* possesses a special *segulah* for longevity, as our Sages, of blessed memory, state:[9] "Whoever puts on *tefillin* merits a long life." Consequently, this is not a religious matter alone, but protection from danger and peril.

[Explain to him that] he is to put on *tefillin* scrupulously [while in the hospital,] regardless of his circumstances concerning the daily performance of Torah and *mitzvos* while at home.

No doubt you will find the right words with which to convey the above; if necessary, translate what I just wrote into English. ...

(*Igros Kodesh*, Vol. IV, p. 301)

ASSISTING OTHERS DURING ONE'S HOSPITAL STAY

It would be most appropriate to utilize your hospital stay to benefit other patients as well.

We know not G-d's ways; possibly this, [i.e., your being of assistance to others,] is the ultimate reason and the main purpose of your hospital stay — and when you will fulfill your main mission in a goodly manner, the secondary aspect, [i.e., your

---

9.   *Menachos* 44a.

health,] will improve as a matter of course, since a secondary aspect always follows the course of the primary aspect, [meaning, by fulfilling your primary reason for being there (helping others), your health will improve as well].

(*Igros Kodesh*, Vol. VI, p. 222)

HELPING OTHERS DURING ONE'S HOSPITAL STAY

Surely I need not encourage you [that during your hospital stay] you should draw those patients who are with you in the hospital closer to our Father in Heaven, doing so in a manner of *ahavas Yisroel*, as taught to us by our Rebbeim and *Nesiim*, of blessed memory.

When one assists in enhancing the spiritual health of a fellow Jew, G-d rewards that person "measure for measure, but many times more so" with good physical and spiritual health. ...

(*Likkutei Sichos*, Vol. XXXVI, p. 296[10])

INQUIRIES FROM RELATIVES
MAKES FOR BETTER HOSPITAL CARE

I received your *pidyon nefesh* for your mother ... *tichye*.

You need to be strong in your *bitachon* in G-d that He will help and that your mother's health will improve. It is important to assure that she is under the supervision of doctors; if she is in a hospital then she certainly is.

From time to time inquire [of the hospital staff] how your mother is doing; the very act of making this inquiry will have an effect on the hospital staff. When they see that people are concerned with her welfare, it will enhance their attitude towards her.

(*Igros Kodesh*, Vol. V, p. 145)

---

10. From a letter of the Rebbe, dated 13 Menachem Av, 5714.

CHAPTER 14

The Health Care Provider

THE PROFESSION OF MEDICINE

... Of all professions, that of a medical doctor calls for the greatest sense of responsibility and meticulousness, and requires the utmost peace of mind to cope with the everyday challenges of the profession.

The Torah holds it in great esteem, considering the human doctor to be the direct agent of the "Healer of all flesh and Performer of wonders" to bring cure and relief both physically and spiritually, as the physical and spiritual go hand-in-hand. ...

(From a letter of the Rebbe, dated the 11th of Tammuz, *erev Chag HaGeulah*, 5744)

PREVENTIVE MEDICINE

... The connection between medicine and Jewish law is found in Torah itself, as our Sages, of blessed memory, declare: "Torah brings healing to the world."

This in no way implies that Torah [which itself brings healing] negates medicine in any way; on the contrary, the Torah establishes that in matters of health, one should consult a doctor and obey his instructions.

Understandably, at the same time [that a person uses the services of a doctor,] the person is to remember that G-d is the true Healer, and the doctor is no more than an agent of G-d, the "Healer of all flesh and Performer of wonders."

There are two fundamental approaches to medicine: a) healing through finding a cure; b) preventive medicine.

The first approach involves active intervention when a health problem is brought to the attention of a doctor, while the second approach — and this has become increasingly prevalent in modern times — strives to achieve the maximum degree of public health by seeking to prevent ailments through inoculations, proper public and private hygiene, a nutritional diet, and by other ways and measures.

It goes without saying that while there is no escaping the need to be healed when one is already ill, preventive medicine is the ideal. Long range, it surely is the most desirable, any way you look at it, including cost, not to mention [its role in] preventing illness and suffering, may G-d protect us.

Additionally, preventive medicine does not require the kind of resources needed to perform extreme measures such as surgery, something that is sometimes unfortunately necessary when healing someone with an existing condition.

In order for preventive medicine to be most beneficial, it requires that one commence prevention at the earliest possible age, beginning with vaccinations, brushing one's teeth to prevent cavities, a balanced diet, and so on.

With regard to Jewish children, preventive medicine also includes scrupulous observance of the laws of kosher food and drink, as it is known how this matter affects the Jewish child's spiritual and physical development. ...

(From a letter of the Rebbe, dated the 15th of Tammuz, 5746)

PRACTICING PREVENTIVE MEDICINE

... Medicine ... has two general aspects: cure and prevention. The first involves curing the sick; the second, preventing illness.

At first glance, the accomplishment of the physician in healing the sick seems more impressive — by yielding such dramatic results — than does practicing preventive medicine, where there can be the illusion that the illness may somehow have been avoided anyway.

In truth, however, [rather than having to combat an illness,] it is surely better to insure against it [from the outset]. The latter [form of healing] is the way G-d practices healing, as it is written:[1] "No illness shall befall you, for I am G-d your Healer."

(From a letter of the Rebbe, dated the 10th of Cheshvan, 5734)

PAYMENT AND GRATITUDE TO A PHYSICIAN

At the outset, on behalf of Mrs. Schneerson as well as on my own behalf, I wish to convey our sincere appreciation for your kind and considerate care in connection to the recent incident that occurred with Mrs. Schneerson. [Thank you] for your immediate response and home visitation at an inconvenient hour, etc., [and] all this in addition to your having provided her with your expert and skilled treatment and care.

I surely need not stress to you how important it is to the patient that the doctor expresses personal interest and attention, particularly as this constitutes a significant aspect in the patient's healing. As you yourself correctly noted in the course of our conversation, the mind has a critical degree of influence over the entire body and one's state of mind directly affects the healing process.

We extend our thanks in anticipation as well of your continued interest and assistance.

I hope and pray that G-d, "Healer of all flesh and Performer of wonders," will bless you with success regarding all your patients, including this present one.

---

1.   *Shemos* 15:26.

I had occasion to hear a thought from my father-in-law, may the memory of a *tzaddik* be for a blessing — a thought that has its place in our Torah, which is called the Torah of Life (as it serves as our guide and source of life) — that in order to assure the success of the medical treatment, the remuneration for the doctor's services are to be in keeping with the medical stature of the treating physician.

In point of fact, this principle applies to all professions and services, including communal services. It need not be said that my father-in-law put this into practice and I wish to do the same.

I therefore am taking the liberty to enclose my check, although I am not sure whether this is the appropriate payment. I am sure, however, that if this sum does not suffice, you will see to it that your secretary contacts my secretary so that I will be able to rectify the matter. Together with the payment comes the traditional Jewish blessing, "Use it in good health."

One of the primary reasons for the above principle is the fact that the Torah is aware that a doctor or someone with another occupation has fiscal responsibilities to his family and community, etc., responsibilities that he can adequately take care of only if his services are adequately paid for.

Therefore, if the receiver of the services does not satisfactorily reimburse the provider of the service, a thought might arise in the doctor's mind (fleeting as it might be) that it would be acceptable for him next time to delay treating this individual in favor of an individual who pays what is expected of him.

Consequently, the Torah strives to remove even the possibility of such a thought. Thus, whatever occupation Providence had in mind for an individual to carry out for the benefit of others, this will always be done with total dedication and devotion.

Once again, my great thanks. With respect and personal regards,

P.S. After this letter was written, your official bill was received. Enclosed please find a check. However, as I emphasized, this is a formal payment while my letter and the [other] attached payment are on a personal basis, as a much deeper and more personal gesture than that of the formal relationship between doctor and patient.

(From a letter of the Rebbe, dated *erev Rosh Chodesh* Shvat, 5743)

THE DOCTOR AS G-D'S EMISSARY

It pleases me to hear from ... about your kind concern and attitude in treating him, particularly the consideration you are showing to all his needs.

There is the known saying of our Sages,[2] of blessed memory, that while giving charity to a poor person is rewarded with "six blessings," when done with a cheerful countenance the donor is rewarded with "eleven blessings."

Together with the known directive of our Sages in commenting on the verse "and he shall heal,"[3] that "Permission was granted the healer to heal,"[4] there was also the concern that people may be led to believe and rely entirely on the doctor and forget that healing is ultimately in G-d's hands. Indeed, according to many commentaries, this is why "Chizkiyahu hid the Book of Cures."[5]

However, when the doctor himself knows that he serves as the emissary of G-d, the "Healer of all (ailments of the) flesh and

---

2.   *Bava Basra* 9b.
3.   *Shemos* 21:19.
4.   *Berachos* 60a.
5.   *Ibid.* 10b; *Pesachim* 56a.

Performer of wonders," there is no room for the above concern, and consequently, his healing is more effective.

May G-d grant you success and bless you in your practice of medicine, that you be the appropriate emissary to bring healing to the afflictions of those individuals who are directed by Divine providence to you.

May G-d reward your good deeds in a similar manner, that your personal matters as well be crowned with blessing and success. ...

(Igros Kodesh, Vol. VII, p. 209)

THE PHYSICIAN AS HEALER OF BODY AND SOUL

... You no doubt conduct yourself in the same manner as do other G-d-fearing doctors, that when patients approach you and seek your advice regarding physical health matters, you utilize the opportunity to rouse them to increase their spiritual health as well — something we are all in need of, particularly in this spiritually impoverished generation, for as the verse states:[6] "There is no man so wholly righteous on earth that he [always] does good and never sins."

The above is particularly true as we readily observe that increased spiritual health leads to a genuine increase in physical health as well, in keeping with the verse,[7] "Be whole with G-d, your L-rd" — whole in the 248 organs and 365 veins of both body and soul, which correspond to the 248 Positive Commandments and the 365 Negative Commandments. ...

(Igros Kodesh, Vol. XV, p. 149)

---

6.   *Koheles* 7:20.
7.   *Devarim* 18:13.

DUTIES OF THE RELIGIOUS PHYSICIAN

I was pleased to be informed of your Conference, designed to create an organized body of Jewish religious physicians.

Unification of religious forces has always been desirable, especially in our generation, a generation confused and perplexed by the shattering events of recent years, as a result of which many thinking people have become completely disillusioned in the false ideas and ideologies which they had held in the past, and are now earnestly searching for the truth.

An organized body of religious physicians could make its influence felt in these circles through a declaration of its authoritative opinion on several issues which have been the subject of confused and misleading controversy.

Such a declaration should, first of all, do away with the misconception about any conflict between science and religion. True science, the object of which is the truth and nothing but the truth, can lead to no conclusions that are contrary to our Torah, the Law of Truth.

On the contrary, the more deeply one delves into science, the stronger must grow the recognition of the truth of the fundamental principles, as well as the ramifications, of our Jewish religion.

As physicians, in particular, you are in a position to refute decisively the path of materialism, as is demonstrated by the fact that so much of physical health depends on spiritual health.

If in the past, emphasis was placed on *"mens sana in corpore sana,"*[8] in our days it is an accepted principle that even a small spiritual defect causes grievous physical harm. The healthier the spirit and the greater its influence over the physical body — the greater its ability to correct or overcome physical shortcomings.

---

8.   "A healthy spirit in a healthy body."

This is to the extent that even in many instances which involve physical healing, prescriptions and drugs are considerably more effective if they are accompanied by the patient's strong will and determination to cooperate [and become well]. ...

The principle of form (quality) over matter (quantity) is further emphasized by the fact— a fact that is continually gaining recognition — that the vital functions of the organism do not depend on quantity, since the glands and their production of hormones and vitamins, etc., are quantitatively quite minute.

Parenthetically: It is written in our Holy Scriptures, "From my flesh I see G-d."[9]

When one recognizes the dominion of the soul in the physical body (the microcosm), there remains but a small step to the recognition of G-d, the "Soul" of the universe (the macrocosm). And in the words of our Sages: "As the soul fills the body, vivifies it, and sees but is not seen — so the Holy One, blessed is He, fills the world, vivifies it, and sees but is not seen."[10]

So much for speaking in general terms. Specifically, there are many questions directly relating to the practice of the physician, many of them of practical importance to the physician, and among them many that relate to practical Jewish law, on which your voice should be heard.

To mention a few:

To publicize the tremendous benefit derived from the observance of the laws of *Taharas HaMishpachah*, observing the laws of family purity, the observance of the dietary laws, and circumcision.

With regard to the genital organs: Elimination of treatment likely to cause sterility and substituting for it other forms of

---

9.   *Iyov* 19:26.
10. *Midrash Tehillim* 103:5.

treatment; particularly, in connection with surgery on the prostate.

Prescription and drugs: Many of them could be made in compliance with the laws of *kashrus*, and only through indifference or carelessness is it not done so.

Post-mortem: For the purpose of the study of anatomy, etc., surely it is possible to use artificial forms and models. For purposes of ascertaining the cause of death — in many cases it is not essential. Where it may be of immediate necessity in order to save a life (as in the case of exonerating someone accused of poisoning by performing an autopsy, etc.) bodily incisions should be reduced to the essential minimum, and all parts of the body should be buried afterwards.

And there are many other similar issues.

Needless to say, what has been mentioned above about pointing out the health benefits that are derived from the observance of the religious precepts should not be understood as an attempt to explain the precepts by describing their benefits.

Divine precepts must be observed because they are the command and will of our Creator, and "the reward of a *mitzvah* is the *mitzvah* itself,"[11] for "this is the whole purpose of man"[12] — to bond and unite with his Maker through the fulfillment of His commands.

However, for the benefit of those who, by reason of spiritual "sickness," cannot be induced to observe the precepts except by making them aware of their practical benefit, we must do everything possible to urge them to observe the *mitzvos* in daily life, even if we have to make rationalizations about the Divine commands by emphasizing their physical benefits.

(*Igros Kodesh*, Vol. XI, p. 202)

---

11. *Avos* 4:2.
12. *Koheles* 12:13.

THERAPEUTIC BENEFITS
OF DOCTOR'S CONCERN FOR PATIENT

I received your letter of the 19th of Tammuz, and I appreciate your thoughtfulness in writing to me in detail about our esteemed mutual friend. No doubt you have already heard from your patient, who has kept in touch with me.

I am most gratified to note the personal attention and concern you have shown towards your patient. There is certainly no need to emphasize to you how important it is for the patient — therapeutically as well — to know that his doctor is taking a special interest in him.

This is all the more important in the case of a sensitive person, and especially as our mutual friend is truly an outstanding person who lives by the Torah, and particularly by the great Torah principle of "loving one's fellow as one loves himself." ...

(From a letter of the Rebbe, dated *Rosh Chodesh* Menachem Av, 5743)

HEALING THE BODY
AND ENCOURAGING THE SPIRIT

... I'd like to take this opportunity to thank you for your devoted care of the *Rabbanis tichye.* According to her you significantly buoyed her spirits.

May G-d will it that in the future as well, you not only heal the bodies of your ill patients but also provide them with encouragement and strengthen their faith and trust in G-d.

(*Igros Kodesh,* Vol. IV, p. 444)

AFFECTION, CARE AND CONCERN OF THE PHYSICIAN

... From the style of your writing it would seem that you are caring for ... not only in the formally prescribed manner of a physician, but also with affection and care and concern —

something that is of vital importance to the course of treatment and healing.

(From a letter of the Rebbe, in the year 5730)

ASSISTING IN A CHEERFUL
AND ENCOURAGING MANNER

It pleased me to receive regards from you in a letter from … who also related to me the kind concern and attention you show her and her entire family, and how you do all this with a cheerful countenance and so on.

There is the known saying of our Sages,[13] of blessed memory, that while giving assistance to another is extremely wonderful, it is ever so many more times so when this aid is provided in a cheerful and encouraging manner.

Surely I need not go on at length about this to an individual like you, who occupies himself in the healing arts, that the personal rapport and empathy of the doctor is influential to the success of the treatment and the confidence and trust [placed in the doctor] by the patient who turns to him, and so on. …

(Igros Kodesh, Vol. XXV, p. 14)

HEALING BODY AND SOUL
IN AN EMPATHIC MANNER

This is to acknowledge receipt of your letter in which you describe the health condition of [your patient] Mr. … . I enjoyed your letter and, most particularly, it pleased me — as I discerned from your way of writing — that you are treating him with genuine warmth and empathy.

Although such conduct, [i.e., treating one's patients with warmth and empathy] is to be expected of all physicians,

---

13. Bava Basra 9b.

unfortunately this is not always the case. Many physicians treat their patients in a more detached and aloof manner, and even among those doctors who are more empathetic — there are many degrees of empathy, caring and concern.

Seeing how you treat your patients with such warmth and empathy encourages me to think that you will rise to even greater degrees of feeling toward your patients. This, in turn, will have an even greater beneficial effect on your patients.

... Surely I don't need to draw your attention to the fact that the spiritual and physical are connected to each other. Medical science also recognizes that the health of the body is linked to the health of the spirit and soul — and not only to the spirit in the simple sense, but also to the Divine soul.

It is therefore my hope that when you heal your patients, you also pay attention to their spiritual state and that you endeavor to heal also their Divine soul — not only their physical body and animal soul.

Even if some of your patients do not feel the necessity [of spiritual healing] and may even be opposed to it — this itself serves as a true sign of how much they are truly in need of this form of healing.

(*Igros Kodesh*, Vol. XIV, p. 386)

THE KIND AND CONSIDERATE HEALER

... At this time it is my pleasant duty to express my thanks for the medical treatment you extended to ..., particularly for the thoughtfulness and empathy you and your staff demonstrated towards him. Surely I need not explain to you how important it is for a patient to be treated by his doctor in a considerate and kind manner.

Although "The reward of a *mitzvah* is the *mitzvah* itself,"[14] [i.e.,] the satisfaction of the doctor in fulfilling his task of healing the ill, and so on, it is also my obligation and a *mitzvah* that is incumbent upon me to express my pleasure concerning the reports that I have received [about your manner of treatment].

May it be G-d's will that since we are living in a period when, for the time being, there are very many who are in need of healing in general, and particularly in the field of your expertise, healing the eyes, that you succeed in bringing about their healing, up to and including their complete healing.

(Igros Kodesh, Vol. XXV, p. 80)

SENDING A MEDICAL REPORT
TO A RENOWNED RESEARCH INSTITUTE

... I completely fail to understand why the doctor who is treating your friend refuses to send a report of her medical condition to the research institute in Washington.[15]

If, as you write, the reason is that they have not discovered the cure there: 1) What would he lose by sending the report to them? 2) How can he possibly know what has been transpiring in that institution of late? As known, it can take many months (and sometimes a year and longer) until such institutions publicize the results of their research.

I can discern only one reason [for his behavior]: that on a psychological level, he does not want to give your friend false hope. But this can be remedied by not informing her that he is sending his report to the institution.

(Likkutei Sichos, Vol. XXXVI, p. 278[16])

---

14. *Avos* 4:2.
15. In all probability, the National Institute of Health.
16. From a letter of the Rebbe, dated 5 Adar Sheni, 5725.

HEAL — BUT DO NOT DECLARE THAT A
NEGATIVE PROGNOSIS MUST INEVITABLY OCCUR

In commenting on the expression of our Sages, "Permission was granted the healer to heal,"[17] the *Tzemach Tzedek* ... noted:

"He has permission to heal, but not — Heaven forbid — to bring about a crestfallen spirit" [by being the bearer of disastrous tidings that *must* inevitably occur], etc.

(Igros Kodesh, Vol. XV, p. 187)

"WHAT EVERY DOCTOR SHOULD KNOW"

... You should also try to influence your brothers *sheyichyu* that they, too, put on *tefillin* daily (aside from *Shabbos* and *Yom Tov*).

Explain to your brother, [the doctor,] that as a doctor, he surely knows how much spiritual health impacts physical health, as the health of the soul affects one's sense of well-being, enabling the person to be resilient and in good spirits.

Being a doctor, he is surely also aware of numerous medications and methods of treatment that are very effective, although doctors do not know how and why they heal. Nevertheless, [i.e., notwithstanding the lack of understanding as to how and why the medications and treatments are effective,] they are utilized, for we recognize that they are of benefit and assistance.

The same is true regarding Torah and *mitzvos*: It is not understanding [the how's and why's of their effectiveness] that is most important, but the actual acts [of studying Torah and performing *mitzvos*].

... A person should not make conditions with G-d, the greatest Healer of all, that first he must understand how His

---

17. *Berachos* 60a.

"medications" [of Torah and *mitzvos*] work, and only then will he swallow the medicine.

Rather, just as trust is placed in the doctor and professor, so too must a Jew's approach to Torah and *mitzvos* be in a similar manner. Doing so will make for a healthy Jew, both in soul and in body.

(Igros Kodesh, Vol. V, p. 183)

A DOCTOR'S RESPONSIBILITY
ALSO EXTENDS TO THE SPIRITUAL

In reply to your letter in which you write that you are pleased with the neighborhood into which you have recently moved, as it possesses many attributes of Torah, *Yiras Shamayim* and *Chassidus* as well.

Surely you and your wife *tichye* are doing your part to enhance these matters, for a neighborhood is anchored by the individuals who are found there and are active in its affairs. Each and every man and woman [residing in the neighborhood thus] has a specific and important role to play to insure its status as a viable neighborhood.

This is particularly so since you are a doctor, and in present times all agree [and doctors know this better than others] that physical health depends on the health and tranquility of the spirit.

There is also the well-known saying of our Sages[18] regarding the peace that is accomplished in this world through Torah, i.e., living a life in harmony with the dictates of the Torah, which — as the Alter Rebbe, author of the *Tanya* and *Shulchan Aruch* explains — refers to the peace between man's Divine and animal soul.

Surely you can find the appropriate words, in harmony with your patients' natures, to also explain to them matters relating to

---

18. *Sanhedrin* 99b.

healing of the soul — explanations that are found in many places, among them *Shemoneh Perakim* of the *Rambam*, as well as *sefarim* of *Chassidus* and *Mussar*. ...

(*Igros Kodesh*, Vol. XIII, p. 488)

HEALING BODY AND SOUL
AND PREVENTING AND ELIMINATING DISEASE

... In keeping with your position as the director of the Medical Association, I extend to you a special blessing that you succeed in utilizing your talents to bring cures and healing to all who turn to you in this regard.

Additionally, and this is of primary importance, that you and your colleagues succeed in eliminating and preventing disease to the extent that healing becomes unnecessary — the ultimate achievement of realizing good health.

Surely — in light of what you write and what I have heard about you — it is superfluous to emphasize that the physical health of all people is connected to their spiritual health, and particularly so with regard to each and every individual Jew.

It is therefore my hope that you are influencing the members of your association to do all they can regarding all those who turn to them, that their patients succeed in possessing healthy souls within healthy bodies.

This is in accordance with the directive of our Torah, the Torah of Life, and its commandments, concerning which the verse states:[19] "You shall live by them," [and as it is also stated:[20]] "For they are our life and the length of our days." ...

(From a letter of the Rebbe, dated the 6th of Iyar, 5732)

---

19. *Vayikra* 18:5.
20. Text of the evening prayer.

USING THE SERVICES OF A NON-JEWISH DOCTOR

... You ask my opinion about going to an excellent non-Jewish medical practitioner — one who has a good name among Jews as well:

[Surely you should go see him, and] I don't understand your reservations, for with regard to healing, no distinction is made [between a Jewish and non-Jewish doctor. This is particularly so in light of the fact that] "An artisan will [perform his work honestly, and] not blemish his work."

Even our *Nesiïm* conducted themselves in this manner [of going to non-Jewish doctors]. Especially so since [in your case] — as you write — the doctor is a religious person.

May G-d send His "healing words" through [the channel] of "this specific doctor and this particular form of treatment."

(Igros Kodesh, Vol. XI, p. 127)

A CAUTION TO PHYSICIANS

... Hospitals and even convalescent centers provide specific regimens of diet, rest and medication in order to heal or strengthen the health of an individual who currently is or recently was unwell.

It is self-understood that such a regime is entirely unsuitable for healthy individuals. On the contrary, such a regimen can make healthy individuals unwell, even dangerously ill, although this very regimen is good and beneficial to those who are ill. For, as we know, there are many medications that are actually extremely toxic but can be extremely valuable when given in minute doses to an individual with a specific ailment.

Someone who is completely healthy does not need to have explained to him or be warned against following the regimen of a hospital or a convalescent center.

This does, however, have to be explained to someone who is not entirely well, or to one who had been ill and became used to such a course of therapy, as it is possible that such an individual will conduct himself in the aforementioned manner even after he becomes well. Such an individual must have explained to him the dangers inherent in such conduct.

Doctors as well, seeing as they do the benefits that patients receive in hospitals and the efficacy of medications in helping to save so many lives, have to be reminded that this manner of conduct is only for those who are ill and not for those who are healthy. For those who are well, the opposite is the case [as mentioned above].

Just as doctors are obliged to provide medication to those who are ill, they are equally obliged to explain to their patients that when they become healed from their maladies they are to completely distance themselves from their previous manner of conduct, [i.e., the taking of medications, etc.].

Only when physicians act accordingly can they be considered proper doctors and healers who fulfill their obligations regarding the sick not only [by assisting them] in the present, but also [by helping prevent medical misfortune] in the future.

Doctors have to be vigilant with regard to the above in respect to themselves as well:

Since they are occupied with healing the ill by providing medications, diet regimens, and so on, and even during their free time they are aware that soon they will have to engage in this once again, this habitual conduct may lead them to mistakenly believe that such behavior, [e.g., taking certain medications,] would be beneficial for them as well; that they too should conduct themselves in this manner.

Doctors should therefore be alert to the possibility [that they may erroneously follow such regimens], [and instead] be constantly aware that such conduct only pertains to those whose health situation calls for such conduct [of taking medications, etc.,] and while doctors are permitted and empowered to assist those who are ill, the doctor himself — if he is healthy — is to conduct himself as healthy people do.

(*Likkutei Sichos*, Vol. XIII, p. 235[21])

DUTIES OF A PHARMACIST

... As soon as a person enters a well-stocked pharmacy, he will observe a vast number of remedies and medications that assist in healing many sick people, even those who are very seriously ill. Understandably, this arouses a feeling of awe in the person who beholds this.

Nevertheless, the pharmacist must explain to that person, and even more importantly, to explain to himself, that all these medications are merely a preparation for healing. In order for the person to be healed, though, two crucial factors are necessary:

An expert in the field needs to indicate which particular medicine, how much, and when that medication is to be taken by the patient. But even this is of no avail if the patient will not actually take the medication; [efforts must be made to assure that the patient does so and is healed].

(*Igros Kodesh*, Vol. III, p. 145)

---

21. From a *sichah* of the Rebbe, dated *Yud-Beis* Tammuz, 5717.

מוקדש

לחיזוק ההתקשרות
לכ"ק אדמו"ר נשיא דורנו

ולזכות

הילדה **חנה פערל** שתחי'

נולדה כ"ט כסלו, ה'תשס"ד

ולזכות אחי'

שלום אליעזר, מנחם מענדל ויונה מרדכי שיחיו

נדפס על ידי הוריהם

הרה"ת ר' **משה אהרן צבי** וזוגתו מרת **העניא רבקה רות**

שיחיו לאורך ימים ושנים טובות

וייס